# Would You Follow You?

Gwen Chermack Hartzler

Prologue

Gwen Chermack Hartzler

# PROLOGUE

***"Write the vision and make it plain on tablets, so he may run who reads it."***

***Habakkuk 2:2***

That is one of my favorite scriptures. I like the concept that whoever is accomplishing the vision is RUNNING to do so. There is an urgency implied. If you want to accomplish something – anything – you must make the vision plain AND you must move quickly with strong forward motion.

The people who are standing around casually reading about the plan are NOT the people who are actually accomplishing the goal. They are not the ones you need to make it *plain* to.

The runners are the important part of the equation. As leaders, we must cater to the runners, not the readers. The runners are the ones doing the legwork to make things happen.

This book is written for the ones who have already run with a vision; the ones who ran well enough, fast enough, and far enough to become leaders of other runners, as well as the ones who will develop future runners.

"People can be divided into two classes: those who go ahead and do something, and those who sit still and inquire why it wasn't done the other way."

~Oliver Wendell Holmes - Physician and poet

# Chapter 1 – Introduction

When was the last time you volunteered for something and felt truly appreciated and valued for your efforts and unique giftings?

What is the longest you have volunteered with an organization? What kept you there for such an extended period of time?

How long will you continue to offer your time and talents on a project when you don't feel any personal or professional fulfillment in return for your efforts?

What organizations have you 'worked' for where you haven't gotten paid, or have not gotten paid what you were worth, but have gladly worked for them anyway?

Have you ever joined a network-based marketing business and felt used, trampled on, ignored, or useless?

In what ways do you show appreciation, and how do others make you feel appreciated?

What is it that keeps people volunteering and drives them to go above and beyond for an organization, a cause, or a person?

The answers to those questions hold the keys to what you are about to discover in this book.

Every one of your responses involves leadership, either positive or negative. When you think about your own past volunteer activities and whether or not they were fun, fulfilling, or rewarding, it can come down to a question of whether you felt that the leadership was worth following or not.

Rarely do the answers to questions such as those hinge on the organization itself. The responses are nearly always directly in reference to the people, and specifically about those in charge. Many times, we give either negative or positive feedback, but cannot put our finger on why we feel the way we do about our time with that group. We just innately know that things were right, or things were wrong.

I will assume that since you are reading this book either you are already a leader or are planning to become a leader, and the real question that needs to be answered is whether you would follow yourself or not.

Are you a person of integrity? Are you teachable? Are you a hard worker and not prone to laziness or procrastination? Are you a person of your word? Are you an encourager? Are you selfish? Do you think of others before yourself?

Would YOU follow YOU?

## ****** VOLUNTEERISM *****

Volunteerism is a wonderful thing. Most people donate their time to at least one organization, and many offer their services for multiple causes. Our lives, our country, and our families have all benefited from their selflessness.

Amazing monuments, tremendous programs, outstanding organizations, and efficient systems have all been conceived, planned, built, funded, and maintained by volunteers. You don't have to look far to find something you use on a regular basis, or somewhere you visit frequently, that was the outcome of volunteer vision and labor.

Community gardens, soup kitchens, churches, homeless shelters, medical clinics, food banks, pregnancy centers, scouting programs, missions outreaches, youth camps, political movements, veterans support, and a myriad of other programs are powered by unpaid or vastly underpaid staff.

Within the world of network marketing, your new recruits are basically volunteers until they start making enough money to offset the necessary up-front time investment. You probably don't want to refer to them as volunteers, but they definitely see themselves that way, and in most cases their spouses certainly do.

Inevitably, not everything found on these pages will apply to you and your specific situation. For example, pastors have different leadership challenges than network marketers do. Regardless of your leadership capacity, you will find helpful ways to become a better leader and improve your skills. Hopefully you can read it with an intent to "eat the fish and spit out the bones."

Having said that, if you are in a position of leadership within an organization that utilizes a volunteer force, in any capacity, this book will be a useful tool for the future of your team.

11

Gwen Chermack Hartzler

# Chapter 2 – My story

When speaking to a group of people, I generally like to start my own personal story with, "I was born at a very young age..." and go from there. Today, I won't go back quite that far.

My volunteer journey began when I was a child. I helped in the church nursery and played on the worship team during services. In my teen years, I worked with the youth group in a leadership position, hosted workshops, started and trained drama teams, continued to play and sing on the worship team, volunteered for leadership positions at summer and winter camps, participated in over 20 short-term missions trips, and pretty much threw my hand in the air any time a volunteer was requested. As an adult, I have continued with many of those activities.

In my 20s, I had my first real taste of volunteer management when I was asked to lead the worship team. I found myself in the position to be the one making the schedules and plans, trying to communicate effectively, being overly diplomatic so as not to upset anyone, and working to keep the other musicians on the team satisfied.

Despite my years as a volunteer on the 'other side of the fence,' it was surprisingly difficult on the leadership side. Just as in any pursuit, it is very easy to 'judge' your leaders and criticize them without the perspective of being able to see the whole picture. I had suddenly become privy to all of the things on the backside of the equation that the volunteers (and/or employees) rarely get to see. There was more to it than I thought.

In my 30s, I began volunteering with the Friends of NRA program to raise grant money for youth shooting sports. After six years of helping out, I was named Volunteer of the Year for the state of Colorado. Later that year, I accepted a position with the National Rifle Association to lead about 450 fellow like-minded volunteers. We hosted 25 annual fund-raising banquets, and raised over $500,000 (net) per year for the NRA Foundation. Definite challenges arose with managing that many people. Just the idea of scheduling around all of their lives, plus having up to a six hour drive – each way - to reach many of them, presented abundant opportunities for personal growth.

Over the years, I have also been involved in several multi-level, direct sales, and network-marketing companies. I have done well with some, yet others haven't even worked out to $1 per hour for my time. Despite consistent talk of *potential* income, I did not earn much. In retrospect, I certainly consider myself to have been a very dedicated 'volunteer' at some of those organizations.

Recently, I have donated my time and talents as a graphic artist, sign maker, and web designer to many of our local churches and ministries, as well as having served on the board of directors for our thrift store and ministry to the homeless and under-privileged in my hometown. In addition, I am still the worship leader at our church.

Having spent many years as a volunteer and many years as a volunteer manager, I have seen the beautiful, the outstanding, the inspiring, the good, the bad, and the downright ugly from both sides of the aisle.

Unfortunately, some leaders have mistreated me and did not value or utilize my giftings, however, most have been sincere in their efforts to be strong and solid leaders. Many have lacked the proper training, yet they have certainly done the best they could. Others have gone above and beyond to show appreciation, earn my loyalty, and retain me on their team.

This book is a compilation of my years of formal leadership training, reading, studying, hands-on learning, and hard-earned insights about how to effectively manage the volunteers we have been given to steward.

Gwen Chermack Hartzler

.

# Chapter 3 – Goal Setting and Accomplishment

Imagine we are setting out on a road trip. We have all the necessary provisions, roadmaps or a GPS, tunes on our iPods, and a supply of Funyuns and Dr. Pepper in the back seat. We get in the car and drive away from the house.

As we are buzzing down the Interstate at 75 MPH, I ask you where we are going. You reply that you have no idea but we are making great time.

How much sense would that make? Maps or a GPS won't do any good at all if we don't know our destination.

> "To be a leader, you have to make people want to follow you, and nobody wants to follow someone who doesn't know where he is going."
>
> ~Joe Namath - Legendary quarterback

So many of us in leadership simply fail to HAVE a vision of what needs to be accomplished. Those who do have a vision, too frequently neglect communicating that goal with their team. We assume they are along for the ride and will go wherever we tell them without a further thought. Would you?

Sometimes, we only give our people bits and pieces of the vision. We get stingy with our directions to them, perhaps out of fear that divulging too much might negate our significance as leaders. That forces the runners (the ones moving forward and accomplishing the vision) to slow down or completely stop while they wait for the next part to be communicated so they can continue to accomplish the goals. That is a failure on the part of leadership.

> "The very essence of leadership is that you have to have vision. You can't blow an uncertain trumpet."
>
> ~Theodore M. Hesburgh
> President of the University of Notre Dame

The concept of a 'team' is a group of people with a shared goal, helping each other to reach that objective, while working together for a common cause. If we don't articulate the goal, vision, or destination, many of them will just plain give up along the way. They will feel like they are spinning their wheels for no good reason.

"Without a vision, the people perish." Proverbs 29:18

Or to paraphrase - without a vision, the project dies because people don't continue to show up.

Imagine for a moment that we are in a huge empty warehouse. I point toward one door at the other end of the building, and tell you to go straight toward that door. While you are focused on getting there, I drop a large wooden crate in front of you. What do you do? You go over or around it and keep heading for the door. Now, let's imagine we are in the same warehouse and I just tell you to walk straight. You ask which direction. I respond that you are intelligent so therefore you can choose. You shrug your shoulders and head out. As you are going in whichever direction you chose, I drop the crate in front of you. What do you do? You stop. OR, you stop, possibly second guess yourself, pause for a time, and make a 90 degree turn proceeding in an entirely different direction.

Obstacles are viewed in a completely different light when our goals are clearly defined. When you know exactly where you are headed and an obstacle is encountered, your own problem solving skills and sense of innovation present themselves. When there is no clear destination, obstacles cause us to completely stop, or at the very least deter us from pursuing the unclear end goal. Most of the time, we cease forward progress.

What can we learn from that concept in reference to accomplishing a goal? **The destination is far more important to communicate than the route is.**

---

"If you're not sure where you are going, you're liable to end up someplace else."

~Robert F. Mager - Author and psychologist

---

# ***** YOUR 'WHY' *****

Simon Sinek, gifted author and speaker, does a fabulous job of explaining why leaders need to start with our WHY before we move on to anything else. I highly recommend that you purchase his materials for a more in-depth look. (www.StartWithWhy.com)

He asserts that the leaders of most organizations do things backward. They start by explaining WHAT they want to do and then HOW they want to do it. The majority never even get around to vocalizing to their own people, let alone the 'customer,' the WHY of their institution.

Within your volunteer organization, the question of WHY absolutely must be answered - as well as communicated effectively - not only to the leadership, but equally as importantly to the volunteer force and the donors.

If your WHY is not well defined - in a way that the people can jump on board with - at the first obstacle you will flounder and most likely fail.

Let's say that you are a high school basketball coach. One day, you decide to start a charity in order to raise funds to build a basketball court in an abandoned parking lot. You tell people WHAT you want to do - build a court – and you tell them HOW you want to do it – through donations and volunteer labor. But what if you don't tell them WHY?

Some will step up to the plate because they like you. Some will join in because they will *assume* what your WHY is and then adopt their own version of your WHY as the truth – leading to major disagreements and disappointments in the future. Some will just want to be part of it in hopes that they can use the court for their own purposes. Most will decline to help.

The big question is WHY do you want to invest all this time and effort to build a court? Is it so young professionals can challenge each other to one-on-one matches outside of their paid gym hours? Maybe it is for the high school team to hold practices outdoors in the sunshine?

OR, is it that you want a place for the underprivileged youth to go so they are outside moving around and not sitting in front of a video game? Maybe you want to volunteer to coach a neighborhood youth league for kids whose parents are still at work when the students get home from school.

Which of those WHYs is compelling and inspirational enough to get volunteers involved and energized? Nothing is wrong with the first two purposes, but very few people are going to be motivated by either of those WHYs.

You will find that people are loyal to your WHY, not to your WHAT or HOW. The WHY is what inspires us to give our blood, sweat, and tears. None of us will go very far above or beyond for the WHAT of an organization. That is not what drives us. That is not what pushes our goals higher and further. That is not what causes us to give up our own time and resources. It's the WHY that motivates.

To illustrate this point, let's look at Mercy Ships. They utilize an impressive volunteer force of medical professionals. Here is what their website says about their WHAT, HOW, and WHY:

*Our Mission: Mercy Ships, a global charity, has operated a fleet of hospital ships in developing nations since 1978. Mercy Ships follows the 2000-year-old model of Jesus, bringing hope and healing to the world's forgotten poor.*

*Our Vision: Mercy Ships uses hospital ships to transform individuals and serve nations, one at a time.*

*Our Values: Desiring to follow the model of Jesus, we seek to:*

> *Love God.*

> *Love and serve others.*

> *Be people of integrity.*

> *Be people of excellence in all we say and do.*

Did you catch their WHY? It's clear in all three of those sections. They want to provide hope and healing. They want to be like Jesus.

Their WHAT is providing free medical care to the poorest of the poor. Their HOW is through a refitted cruise ship parked offshore and staffed by volunteers. But their WHY is what is compelling. It is well defined and people are eager to get on board and be part of their organization.

Your WHY, once it is clearly defined and adopted, should drive your goal setting. Your WHAT is only proof that you believe your WHY. People don't buy into your WHAT. They buy into your WHY.

---

"Discipline is remembering what you want."

~David Campbell - Found of Saks

---

There were three brick-layers building the walls of a structure. A man walked up to the first and asked him why he was laying bricks. "It's my job. I get paid to do this for eight hours a day. I have three hours and 12 minutes left until I get to go home and relax."

He went over to the second man and asked him why he was laying bricks. "This is my career. I've worked hard at it all my life and I'm very good. That's why they hired my company. We'll be finished in about three weeks and then we are on to the next job."

He approached the third man and inquired with the same question. "This is my calling. I'm building a church. A place where people can come and connect with God. Their lives will be forever changed because of each brick I'm putting into this wall. I love doing it and can't wait to see it finished so its doors can be opened and it will be a place of blessing to people!"

Each of those three men had different reasons for doing the exact same task. Only one had a WHY that was big enough for him to love doing it.

**Working hard at something you don't love = stress.**
**Working hard at something you love = passion.**

##### ***** OWNING THE GOALS *****

One thing I learned early was to give my volunteers an outline of my goals, starting with the big picture and working backward to specifics. Once they had some time to digest the broad objective, I asked them to formulate *their own* goals and publicly state them.

I found that almost without exception, theirs were loftier than mine. They set the bar higher than I did. This was especially true of fund-raising projects. We raised much more money by adopting their goals than we would have by maintaining mine.

---

"Start by doing what it necessary, then what is possible, and suddenly you are doing the impossible!"

~St. Francis of Assisi

---

The imperative thing about allowing people – runners - to make their goals public is that then *they* own the goals and they are no longer working to fulfill *your* vision, they are laboring to meet THEIR OWN objectives. That energizes them with high octane fuel in their gas tanks.

If, by some odd chance, they are negative and say no to what you want, either your WHY has not been effectively communicated and they are not on board with it, or they are readers and not runners. They are not the ones you need to cater to. However, if you have done a good enough job of 'selling' your WHY, either the skepticism won't happen, or their peers will quickly help them acclimate.

In addition to the need to illuminate your destination, the main goal needs to be communicated. Your organization is probably alive because it is here to correct an injustice. That is likely your WHY. In one form or another, it is to rectify an inequality. If there was no injustice, there would be no need for your organization.

Homelessness or hunger?  Salvation Army or Rescue Missions
Neglected youth?  Boys and Girls Club
Starving children?  Compassion International
Unexpected pregnancy?  Crisis Pregnancy Centers
Natural disasters in 3rd world countries?  Samaritan's Purse
Concern about people's eternal salvation?  Churches

My husband and I are part of a network-marketing based financial company whose WHY is to help middle class families get out of debt, save money, plan for retirement, and pay less taxes. There is a severe injustice that we are working to correct – the financial illiteracy in the United States has reached epic proportions, and unless you have a substantial portfolio most financial advisors won't give you the time of day. A significant portion of the population has no idea how money works, and therefore they have no concept of how to plan for the future. We help them for free. Even within the world of MLMs, the thought of correcting an injustice stands.

Whether you desire to make medical care more affordable, or if you hope to support abandoned children, or you want to raise money for afterschool youth programs, you are attempting to fix an injustice. That is your WHY.

Be sure to put it into your vision statement. If your teammates can keep in mind that there is an injustice out there, and your team is working hard to correct it, that will give them ownership of the WHY. It will give them a reason to show up for meetings. It will give them the impetus to open their mouths and speak up. It will drive them to RUN toward the destination, not just read about it.

> "It is a useless life that is not consecrated to a great ideal. It is like a stone wasted on the field without becoming a part of any edifice."
>
> ~Jose Rizal - Phillipino revolutionary

In other words, if you aren't involved in something bigger than yourself, you are like a stone that is fit for a grand temple, but lies in a field with all of its beautiful potential wasted.

Interestingly, the word 'consecrated' means to be set apart for some special purpose. Common things are not consecrated. It implies great promise or possibility that needs to be nurtured in a specific direction.

Your WHY is the cornerstone. Your goals will be driven by your WHY. Once the destination is defined, the potential of your teammates will not be wasted and left lying in a field.

## ***** THE POWER OF THE SMALL WIN *****

If I wanted to run the Bolder Boulder, a 10K footrace, I would not-only stay focused on the finish-line, but I would also watch for the kilometer markers lining the way to see how far along I am. As the end of the race draws nearer, my will to finish would increase, even though the effort to continue would most likely escalate as well. My lungs would be burning, my muscles on fire, and with each passing kilometer marker, my resolve would grow stronger. I would be thinking, "I can't quit now! I have come this far and I want to finish well!"

---

"The older I get, the more wisdom I find in the ancient rule of taking first things first; a process which often reduces the most complex human problem to a manageable proportion."

~President Dwight D. Eisenhower

---

Let's assume the goal you and your 'runners' have adopted is a monetary one. You need to raise $25,000 toward the purchase of an ultrasound machine for the local crisis pregnancy center.

They know the destination is $25k, but have absolutely no idea how to accomplish that. You can break it down into several smaller waypoints. Yes, there is a final objective or finish line, but there are markers along the way.

For the sake of this example, we'll break it down the following way:

Fund-raising dinners $10k

Letter writing campaign - $5k

Donations from loyal supporters - $5k

Quilt Raffle - $2k

Radio talk show plea for contributions - $2k

Local churches filling baby bottles with change - $1k

Several of these ideas will take quite some time to accomplish, but you should start with the easiest and fastest one so your teammates begin to build momentum. Once they see forward motion, it will invigorate your runners and give them motivation to continue working toward the hardest projects.

---

*"Any fool can make something complicated.
It takes a genius to make it simple."*

*~Woody Guthrie - Singer/songwriter*

---

HUGE power comes from these small wins. Always celebrate them. Many times they are more important than the end goal in the eyes of your volunteers. Once they know you are paying attention to each step along the road, it will make the accomplishment of every specific mile marker more important and the road to your destination seem shorter and more achievable.

Once you have raised the very first $1000, there should be some sort of celebration with your volunteer workers. They have accomplished the first of many goals and are far less likely to quit running toward the grand total. It can be as simple as showing up to the next meeting with cookies and making a big-deal type of announcement that the first waypoint goal has been met!!! WOO HOOO!

---

"The role of leadership is to transform the complex situation into small pieces and prioritize them."

~Carlos Ghosn
CEO of Renault, Nissan, and Mitsubishi Motors

---

Question: is it easier to change the direction of a motorcycle when it is parked, or when it is moving? Have you ever tried to turn a stationary motorcycle? Without lifting, it's nearly impossible, even if you are strong. Steering it is, of course, a much more achievable task once it is moving, even if that is only at a crawling speed.

Next question: Is it easier to encourage our teammates in a particular direction when they are standing still or when they are moving? It is our first task to get them moving. Forward motion makes the concept of guided leadership actually attainable. Start with small, easily achievable waypoints, and move on from there.

"Great things are not done by impulse, but by
a series of small things brought together."

~Vincent VanGogh - Gifted artist

To illustrate this point: I am a firearms instructor. People are required to take a class like mine in order to obtain a concealed handgun permit. The majority of my students have never fired a handgun before, or have never been instructed how to do it correctly. After about 8 hours of classroom time, we go out to the range. Our first set of targets are at three yards. Three yards. That's about 10 feet. That is mighty close.

However, it is very much intentional. Those students who are either afraid of firearms, or convinced they cannot hit the broad side of a barn, hit very near the center of the target the first time they squeeze the trigger. I see this as a small win, but to these new shooters, it is a huge and motivating win. It propels them forward. We whoop and holler and celebrate their first successful attempts, building their confidence.

By the end of the range day, after we have shifted the shooting line backward by several yards, they are asking if they can keep moving further from the targets just to see how many times they can hit it from a greater distance. The power of the small win has set them up to propel themselves to bigger and better wins. I no longer need to push them. They gladly put the pressure on themselves.

> "A good leader inspires others with confidence
> in him; a great leader inspires them
> with confidence in themselves."
>
> ~President Franklin D. Roosevelt

Any time our runners grab hold of their own vision to succeed, our job will become easier and far more successful. They will be reading it *while* they are running, and will take responsibility for accomplishing it. They will be driven toward the destination by their own WHY!

Setting a goal, getting them to own their part of it, and celebrating the small wins, is a certain recipe for success!

> "If your actions inspire others to dream more,
> learn more, do more, and become
> more, you are a leader."
>
> ~President John Quincy Adams

## ***** GIVE VS GIVE BACK *****

It is good to propose this question to our teammates: "Here's the mountain; how much can you contribute?" That gives them the opportunity to own the

31

results as well as the goal. If they want to give financially, that's fantastic. If they want to give their time, that's excellent. If they want to donate products to make money with, that's wonderful. They do want to contribute, or they wouldn't be there.

As leaders, we need to be sure we are giving them the opportunity to 'give', but not guilting them into feeling like they have to 'give back'. There is a huge difference between those two ideas.

Giving is a generosity driven concept. They *want* to give their time, money, or hard work because they *want* to bless someone or some cause. They *want* to be part of correcting an injustice. They *want* to be involved in some greater purpose.

Giving back is guilt driven. It implies the idea that they owe it to you, to the cause, to society, or to a person. They are no longer doing it out of the goodness of their heart. They are doing it to assuage their conscience. They are being made to feel like they *have* to give in order to be considered a decent human being.

Have you ever heard of buyer's remorse? Well, there is an equally real concept of giver's remorse. People will cancel credit card transactions the next day, put stop-payments on their checks, or call and want their donation back if they are made to feel guilty in the process of giving. They may reluctantly pull out their wallet when pushed, but it will certainly be a one-time donation. The next time, they will avoid you and skip your event completely because they know someone will try to guilt them into 'giving back'. Try your best to avoid that mindset.

"You give little when you give of your possessions. It is when you give of yourself that you truly give."

~Kahlil Gibran
Poet and writer of the The New York Pen League

Gwen Chermack Hartzler

# Chapter 4 – Retention

Is it easier to train someone new or keep the already trained person happy and engaged?

Studies have shown that an $8 per hour employee costs approximately $10,000 to train. At a $40,000 per year position, it is as much as 38% of their annual salary to train them. I realize we are talking about volunteers, not employees, but the point still stands. Your time is valuable. If you make $40,000 per year, you are being paid approximately $20 per hour. How many hours of your time does it take to train someone new?

I know there is the odd blessed volunteer who steps into a role that fits them like a glove and they just take off and soar, but that is the exception rather than the rule. It is a time-consuming and costly thing to recruit and train new people.

I recently read a statistic about why people change jobs. As many as 75% of all people who voluntarily leave their jobs do so because of their BOSSES, not because of the position, the pay, the hours, or even their co-workers. People don't usually quit jobs. They quit bosses, managers, and supervisors.

Imagine how much more applicable that is to volunteerism. There is no monetary reward, only a belief in the WHY to keep them there. If other things override the pleasure in accomplishing something for the cause, they will leave in a heartbeat.

The main goal, as a leader, should always be retention. If our teammates are sticking around for a great deal of time, that is a sign that the program is healthy and we are doing a good job of empowering them.

Those involved in network-marketing (NM) understand that recruiting new people is the basis of their business and future income. Most multi-level-style companies have 'run the numbers' and will give you a figure, on average, of how many people you must talk to before you can get one actual recruit. That number is between 25 and 100. They also estimate between 5 and 15 recruits before you get one who will actually 'stick' and make money from the company. The number of recruits necessary in order to get the three you need to stay and actually do something is in the arena of 50. You will recruit a LOT of readers for each runner you find.

Holy cow! That is an immense amount of time, energy, and resources wasted on recruiting and training people and then having them quit anyway. Those are readers and not runners. Cater to the runners.

---

"Those few who use their strengths to incorporate their weaknesses, who don't divide themselves, those people are very rare. In any generation there are a few, and they lead their generation."

~Moshe Feldenkrais - Israeli physicist

---

The infographics of you recruiting two people, and those two recruiting two people, and before you know it, you have built an empire(!) look great on paper and generally make the 'business' easier to sell to your friends and family. However, NOBODY succeeds in network marketing with only their first two or three personal recruits. It just doesn't work that way.

Statistics show that your first five recruits into a NM or MLM business will quit shortly after signing up, or will go into a 'witness protection program' and avoid you like the plague. It's a funny visual, but it certainly makes a point! They hide from you, or they just plain give up. How sad is that? It is a failure of leadership.

---

"Leadership is the art of giving people a platform for spreading ideas that work."

~Seth Godin - Author, entrepreneur, and speaker

---

So, how do you stop the turn-over cycle that is within your volunteer or MLM organization?

The growth and development of people is the highest calling of any leader. Concentrate on your volunteers - your team - your runners.

You are not responsible for the numbers.

You are not responsible for the results.

You, as the leader, are responsible for the PEOPLE who are responsible for the numbers.

You are responsible for the PEOPLE who are responsible for the results.

That is where your time and effort needs to be concentrated. The PEOPLE.

---

"People cannot be managed. Inventories can be managed, but people must be led."

~H. Ross Perot - Business magnate and politician

---

Be a leader. Don't be a boss, a manager, or a supervisor. Nobody wakes up in the morning wanting to be bossed, managed, or supervised. However, almost everyone is willing to be led.

There are a few basic people skills that every leader needs to work on and cultivate in order to retain their volunteers.

Leaders need to:

- Walk in integrity
- Be able to communicate effectively and connect with their teammates
- Be confident
- Remain focused on the right things
- Encourage, encourage, encourage

I recently heard about a young man in middle school who was 'chosen' to run the one mile race for their track and field day at the end of the year. We will call him Steve. Steve was much more physically suited to throw the shot put than to run a mile, but the teacher told him to line up and run, so he did. He started out with the pack, but quickly ended up 100 yards behind them, then the gap grew to 200 yards and continued to widen. God bless Steve, he persevered, panting the whole time. As he came lumbering past the stands, his mother stood up and yelled, "Run faster, Steve!"

He stopped, turned his face toward her with a look that said, "What do you think I'm doing?!?" collapsed on the track, and began to cry.

Steve's mom did not understand the idea of encouragement, nor that it is likely to be different for each person. Maybe she heard the parents of the athletic kids encouraging their competitive children with those words, and had watched it work. Perhaps she was embarrassed and wasn't sure what to say. Possibly she truly didn't know better and thought her words would help him.

There is a lesson to be learned in this story. Pay attention to your teammates. Some of them need to be encouraged to set their sights higher because they are underestimating themselves. Others need to be told that they can do it, no matter what it looks like to the people around them. Some need to be reminded repeatedly that ANY forward motion, no matter how slow, gets them closer to finishing. They just need to keep moving forward.

The pace is relative to the person who is doing the running. Always try to keep in mind that how you encourage them is as important as the fact that you do it at all. Pressure is a very welcome thing to those who think they have a chance at gaining a competitive edge. That same pressure kills the motivation of those who are struggling to keep moving, or to even begin moving at all.

Gwen Chermack Hartzler

# Chapter 5 – Nuts & Bolts

The following very practical suggestions are the 'nuts and bolts' of this book. They are mostly presented in an ALWAYS and NEVER format because they are pretty cut-and-dried. There are very few exceptions.

If you can master these, you will encourage, develop, equip, and retain your unpaid and underpaid people.

ALWAYS start on time. 9AM means 9AM, NOT 9:05 because you are waiting for more people to show up. 8:45 does not mean 9, either. Have the common courtesy to treat your teammates like adults. If you want to start *AT* 9, tell them so. If you tell them you are going to start at 8:45, hoping that the latecomers will actually be there by 9, all you do is punish your best people, your runners, the ones who behave like adults and show up on time or before.

When you do not start on time every time, you are pandering to the lowest common denominator – the readers - which will not lead to happy 'on time' teammates. The runners are the ones you want to retain, after all.

Your readers will come and go with the breeze, they are flighty at best. But your runners, on the other hand, once they have committed to your WHY, if you respect them with your own punctuality, they will stick with you like gum on your shoe.

After your teammates see you doing what you said you would do (that is integrity) a few times, they will quickly figure out that they need to be at least five minutes early if they want to be on time.

---

"In matters of style, swim with the current. In matters of principle, stand like a rock."

~President Thomas Jefferson

---

ALWAYS treat your volunteers like adults and they will behave like adults. Take care of your best people by treating them well, and they will take care of your cause as well as taking care of you. It is a matter of mutual respect, integrity, and honesty.

Treat people like children, and they will behave like children. Don't give in to the temptation to baby your teammates. If you told them you would be meeting next Tuesday at 7pm, there is no need for you to call each of them on Monday and remind them of the meeting.

They are adults. When you stop expecting them to act like adults, they may revert to child status and no longer take responsibility for their actions. You will hear things like, 'But I didn't get a reminder call, so that's why I didn't show up' or, 'Nobody told me!'

If they are expected to keep track of things on their own, they will learn quickly to pay attention to what is being said because you expect them to. Otherwise, it becomes a vicious cycle of you trying to keep track of everyone. You have much better things to do with your time than call everyone to remind them of a meeting that you told them about last week.

---

"You do not lead by hitting people over the head. That's assault, not leadership."

~President Dwight D. Eisenhower

---

NEVER end ANY conversation without thanking them. You are where you are because of them, and somewhere inside, they know this. Your job or position exists in order to motivate them. Be genuine in your appreciation and recognition, though, because people instinctively perceive a phony attitude. Heartfelt gratitude is possibly the best motivational force out there.

Always, and I do mean *always* tell them how much you appreciate their efforts. Always.

---

"A good objective of leadership is to help those who are doing poorly to do well, and to help those who are doing well to do even better."

~Jim Rohn - Entrepreneur, author, and speaker

---

ALWAYS say please. Be overly diplomatic. You may get away with 'telling them what to do' for a brief period of time, but in the long run, they know you cannot fire them and they do not have to do anything you tell them to do. Adopting a habit of saying 'please' and phrasing everything as a request will cause them to feel needed and valued.

Do you enjoy it when someone in leadership orders you around? Of course not. Nobody likes it. Your volunteer teammates are not your servants, nor are they your employees. They are, however, the most important part of the equation. Remember, you are responsible for the PEOPLE who are responsible for the results. Your task completely revolves around your people, and a little diplomacy is good. A LOT of diplomacy is better!

Have you ever heard the old adage about how you attract more bees with honey than vinegar? It is so true ... especially in the volunteer world.

---

"The reason that most major goals are not achieved is that we spend our time doing second things first."

~Robert J. McKain - Author

---

ALWAYS be crystal clear about what you want/need them to do. If you leave room for misinterpretation, more often than not, it will get misinterpreted.

If you need them to set up 12 tables with red cloths and arrange the silent auction items on the first three only, be very specific with them. "Hey, please set up those tables and get the silent auction stuff on them, would ya?" will get you either two tables or every table in the room. No cloths, or the wrong ones, and boxes of packaged stuff put on top of the tables in the corner. Then you have to waste their time (and yours) to get it done a second time so that it is done how you needed it in the first place. Be specific in the first place and avoid do-overs.

An efficient and effective use of their time and effort will be greatly appreciated by your runners.

If we let them know precisely what we need done, without micro-managing them, they will do everything they can to accomplish our requests … especially if they know we will thank and praise them when they do it well.

---

### "An order that can be misunderstood will be misunderstood."

~Napoleon Bonaparte - Emperor of France

---

ALWAYS have a positive attitude and outlook. If you believe and articulate that they can do something, they will 'borrow your belief' and rise to your expectations. They will literally feed off of your attitude.

I remember in 2009 we were just putting together our big Friends of NRA fund-raising banquet here in town and the state rep, Marc Steinke, came to our meeting. We were all a bit downtrodden and someone told him we might as well not have the banquet because the economy had crashed and nobody had any extra money to spend. Marc shook his head and said that the economy has nothing to do with anything; people will still support the causes they believe in. He politely informed us that he didn't want to hear that excuse come up again. We all borrowed his belief and soldiered on. It ended up being the most successful banquet we ever had up to that point.

We were right, but he was more right. If he would have agreed with us and taken on a defeatist attitude, it could have destroyed the whole program. God bless him for keeping things positive.

---

"You take people as far as they will go, not as far as you would like them to go."

~Jeanette Rankin
The first woman to hold Federal office

---

"We choose to go to the moon. We choose to go to the moon. We choose to go to the moon, in this decade, and do the other things. Not because they are easy, but because they are hard." President John F. Kennedy – September 1962

That speech was given just over a year before he died. When he first articulated that visionary statement in 1961, it was less than three weeks after Alan B.

Shepard had made the *very first* manned US flight and was in space for all of 15 ½ minutes.

There was no technology, no materials, no manpower, no game plan, and no actual way to achieve his dream. Considering it was near the end of 1962, he only gave NASA seven years to accomplish it.

---

"Every technological innovation was once considered impossible by those unwilling to try."

~Keith Borgelt - My highly intelligent uncle

---

However, he put his vision out there, along with the belief that we, as a nation, would be able to succeed. That bold goal not only put 12 human beings on the moon, but it also provided 400,000 people with jobs and gave us things such as modern athletic shoes, Teflon, contemporary firefighting apparatus, solar panels, programmable pacemakers, wireless technology, quartz clocks/watches, and handheld cordless vacuum cleaners.

His WHY was very well communicated to the nation in that speech. After declaring that we wanted to do it because it was hard, and that in itself makes it worthwhile, he went on to state, "….because that goal will serve to organize and measure the best of our energies and skills. Because that challenge is one that we are willing to accept, one we are unwilling to postpone, and one which we intend to win…"

His WHY certainly involved beating the Russians, there is no doubt; however, he was able to communicate a much deeper intention. He wanted us to prove, through the very best of our energies and skills, that absolutely *nothing* was too hard if we put our zeal and cooperation into it.

His WHY resonated with the American people, and they were willing to spend about $32 billion in the quest. That is about $110 billion in today's money. Can you imagine any politician being brash enough to request that much money to accomplish a goal that was nothing more than science-fiction at the time?

Although JFK was really barely involved in getting an American on the moon, he was absolutely instrumental. He was daring in his proclamation and we all borrowed his belief that we were able to do what he envisioned. He is certainly responsible in big part for the success of the NASA program. I believe, in retrospect, that was his crowning achievement.

If you have a grand vision for your program, communicating it with passion and surety will go a long way in getting your team on board. Making certain that it is written plainly so your runners can run while they are reading and accomplishing it is the key. It is okay to dream big, so long as your WHY is big enough to justify it!

---

"A leader is a dealer in hope."

~Napoleon Bonaparte - Emperor of France

---

ALWAYS remember to smile, laugh, and have fun. Nobody wants to give up their free time to go to dry and boring meetings. Nobody. In every situation, that will look a bit different. I tend to tell a joke or two at our worship practice, right off the bat, to get everyone laughing, smiling, and in good moods. That does not always work in a meeting where the subject matter is more serious. However, YOUR smile will be contagious, and will cause others to lighten their mood, even when they do not realize it is happening.

---

"The leadership instinct you are born with is the backbone. Then you develop the funny bone and the wish bone that go with it."

~Elaine Agather - CEO JP Morgan Bank

---

Have you seen the movie 'Risen'? There is a spot where Claudius is interviewing anyone the soldiers can find who had anything to do with Yeshua. They locate Bartholomew and bring him in to answer questions. The guy is just plain full of joy. He smiles the whole time he is being interrogated. I found myself smiling while I was watching him, and turned to see that my husband was smiling as well. Even in a scripted movie, a smile that is sincere is contagious. Make sure yours is in place as often as possible.

A financial company my husband works with has an open meeting room in the center of the office where the training and recognition are done. Everyone in the rest of the office can hear the laughter during the training as well as the applause and cheering for the folks who are doing well. When they moved to a new office building, I told the branch manager how much that laughter and cheering motivated the people 'on the outside' who were hearing it. It makes people want to work with a team like that – either as a client or an associate. Everyone wants to be part of something fun and successful. Their new office location kept that same model, and I think it has had a great deal to do with their company expansion.

You rarely go wrong by promoting good humor. You attract more ants with a lollipop than a stick of celery.

---

"No pessimist ever discovered the secrets of the stars, nor sailed to an uncharted land, nor opened a new heaven to the human spirit."

~Helen Keller - First deaf-blind person to earn a BA degree

---

NEVER waste your teammates' time. Time is our most valuable commodity. It is more precious to productive people than gold. If I want to waste my own time, that is my choice. However, if I volunteer for something and the leadership wastes my time, that is a *whole* different dynamic. Sure, I MAY have only been mindlessly watching TV if I were at home, but that is completely irrelevant. I might have had to give up other important activities in order to attend the meeting. You don't know, nor is it important.

If I make the effort to show up, on time, ready to accomplish something, by golly the leadership had better have their ducks in a row and allow me to use my time for something worthwhile.

Don't be just starting to make copies for them five minutes after you were supposed to begin the meeting.

Don't be on a phone call and leave them doing nothing because they don't have any clear cut direction.

Don't keep the plans to yourself to the point that they can only go so far and then they have to wait for you to give them further instruction.

Allow them to run. Allow them to take off and soar!

---

"Show me a man who cannot be bothered to do the little things, and I'll show you a man who cannot be trusted to do the big things."

~Lawrence D. Bell - Founder of Bell Aircraft

---

NEVER call a meeting or conference call unless you actually have something important to say. There is nothing more disrespectful than making our volunteers bail on family time, cut a meeting short, miss out on another opportunity, or whatever else, just so that we can mark off a checkbox that we had a get-together.

IF you are required to have a meeting or call, do some research and find something important and relevant to share with them. You may want to expound upon the cause (the WHY), you can research new ways to raise funds, or maybe find YouTube videos on how other organizations handle situations similar to yours. Whatever you do, make sure that any time you 'require' from them is well used and informational.

> "Those who follow the part of themselves that is great will become great. Those who follow the part that is small become small."
>
> ~Mencius - Chinese philosopher

Don't waste their time, either in a meeting or during their volunteer activities, by attempting to control or micro-manage, and they will give you as much time as you ask for.

Try your best to not repeat yourself for the sake of one or two new people, or to catch the latecomers up to speed. That is terribly disrespectful to the ones who show up early and often.

If you call a one hour meeting, but are able to cover everything you need to cover in the first 20 minutes, by all means, release them. Every single one of them is as busy as we are, even if it is only in their own perception. The more of their time we take up, the less of it they have to be working for the cause.

However, if you need a full hour, take it, but make sure that what you are keeping them there for brings actual value to the mission. People don't mind if we use their time for something that contributes to the project. Just be very clear about the benefits, so they don't get crabby about it and spread discontent. Everyone is more likely to remain involved and committed when their time is not being wasted.

Don't exceed the time allotted for the meeting, either. Whether it is a one-on-one or a group meeting, you asked them to give up a certain amount of their precious time. Do everything in your power to be finished when you said you would be finished. If you want your teammates to take you at your word on the big things, prove you mean what you say on the 'little' things – like having integrity where time is concerned.

---

"The quality of a leader is reflected in the standards they set for themselves."

~Ray Kroc - CEO of McDonalds

---

ALWAYS be the first one there and the last one to leave. A good leader is the one who unlocks the door, turns on the lights, starts the heater or A/C so it is comfortable, sets up the chairs, and has the paperwork ready to distribute before the first person even shows up. Unless there are extenuating circumstances, the leader should also always be the last one out the door. Your runners will greatly appreciate your extra effort on this front.

---

"The price of greatness is responsibility."

~Winston Churchill - Prime Minister of the UK

---

ALWAYS work on *connecting* with your teammates, not just communicating with them. Touch base frequently, but don't smother them. A weekly email or group text to give an update is great. Extra conversation to set up meetings and such is necessary, but don't include people who don't need to be included. It wastes their time to be in on emails, group texts, or calls that are irrelevant to them.

On the flip side, don't contact them only when you need something. Nobody wants to feel used. If you can, keep track of their birthdays, anniversaries, or something similar and reach out to them occasionally, when you don't need anything specific. Send a card or a text in celebration. Any time you can personalize the communication, it becomes *connection*, not just communication, and they will feel like part of a team and work harder ... for YOU.

We all know that life is about relationships. Work hardest on those, and the rest of it will come naturally. Remember, you are responsible for the PEOPLE.

---

"True leadership lies in guiding others to success - in ensuring that everyone is performing at their best, doing the work they are pledged to do, and doing it well."

~Bill Owens - Author

---

ALWAYS be careful with setting actual hard and fast requirements. Specific meetings or practices that are <u>truly</u> necessary to success will be generally tolerated. Requiring attendance or time for things that are not actually necessary will lead to higher drop-out rates.

Don't call an 'Emergency Meeting' unless it genuinely is an emergency! You will only get away with that one once. From that point, your credibility is shot, and the next time you will be treated like the boy who cried, 'wolf.'

Be sure to provide many opportunities for them to volunteer and get involved, but allow them to choose <u>when</u> they want to give you their time. If our teammates do not feel pressured, they will give us far more time than they would if we 'required' them to attend, and for a much longer duration.

The ones who go above and beyond are generally your runners. That's an easy way to identify them.

---

"Average leaders raise the bar on themselves; good leaders raise the bar for others; great leaders inspire others to raise their own bar."

~Orrin Woodward - Founder of Life Leadership

---

Repetition. To repeat or not to repeat; that is the question. Yes, repetition is the main way the human brain learns and retains information; however, some things do not need to be repeated in order for that to happen.

There is nothing more frustrating for a runner than to show up, on time, committed to the cause, and hear the same 'drivel' that they heard in the last five meetings. If there are important things that need to be covered ... again ... do it as quickly and sparsely as possible and move on.

Sometimes we will get ONE new person in a group of 25 regulars and the speaker or moderator will start from scratch for that one person. The other 24 people will then tune them out and start building their grocery shopping list. Then, when the speaker talks about something important to the other 24, most of them will miss the new content because their minds have already wandered away.

You are far better to assign one of the veteran members of the team to communicate the basics to the new person in a one-on-one situation, and not waste the time of the other 24 people. They will all be grateful that you respect their time, and the person whom you choose for the task will feel needed and valued. That's a win on both sides.

---

*"I've always found that the speed of the boss is the speed of the team."*

~Lee Iacocca
Legendary executive in the automotive industry

---

Repetition. To repeat or not to repeat; that is the question ... again. There are certain principles that we absolutely MUST get across to our volunteers: ethics, procedures, compliance issues, integrity, paperwork requirements, etc. We must be repetitive about those things. Always.

If one of your volunteers does something that is 'wrong', you will most likely take the heat for it. Making certain they know the rules is a very good thing.

---

"Leadership is a potent combination of strategy and character. But if you must be without one, be without the strategy."

~General Norman Schwarzkopf

---

Rinse - Re-package - Repeat. This concept remains as one of the most important. All of us learn through repetition. That is the way our human brains are wired. Granted, some people require more repetition than others, but the foundation stands.

When your teammates just don't 'get it', that can be resolved in two ways:
- Sometimes you need to figure out how to phrase it differently
- Sometimes, you just need someone else to present the material

Have you ever had a conversation with someone who tries to tell you something, you don't understand what they are asking so you request clarification, and they repeat their exact words to you a second or even a third time? It is incredibly frustrating and counter-productive.

We have to learn how to re-phrase nearly everything we say in order to achieve comprehension from our teammates. If we see them frowning while we talk, staring blankly off in the distance, or fidgeting, that generally means they need us to say it differently, not just repeat it.

We all had teachers in high school who did that. They would write a math equation up on the board and then show you how to solve it. You would raise your hand and say that you didn't understand what they just did, so they would erase that equation and start over with a nearly identical problem and do the same thing they just said and did, with no additional explanation. Then, they would look directly at you and say, "Do you get it now?" Very few of us had the nerve to admit that we still had no idea how they got to the correct answer.

---

"The mediocre teacher tells. The good teacher explains. The superior teacher demonstrates. The great teacher inspires."

~William Arthur Ward - Author

---

If we do not hear our teammates repeating the things we are teaching them, either to us or to others, it means they may not be getting what we are attempting to instill in them.

Sometimes it takes several rinsed, re-packaged, and repeated messages for them to even hear it one time clearly.

Other times, they seemingly hear what you are saying, but for whatever reason, they do not apply it to their life. They have heard you say the same thing many times, but it does not register, no matter how many times you have rinsed, re-packaged, and repeated it. They have become 'parent deaf'.

You bring in someone else, not the person who has poured so much into them (read YOU), not the one they hear day after day - week after week (read YOU), and suddenly the light goes on! They actually heard what the other person said, took it to heart, and applied it to their life. The other person may have literally said the exact same thing you did, word for word, but they are praised as a genius and their advice is immediately taken wholeheartedly.

Sometimes that hurts, but parent deafness happens to the best of us. It is okay. Please don't ever feel like you are the only one who should or could talk and explain a particular concept. Others are certainly capable, and sometimes get the point across much better than you ever could, due to YOUR people not hearing YOUR voice on a subject.

We need to swallow our pride and allow others to speak into the lives of our teammates. If we truly want to help them grow and succeed, no matter how difficult this may be, we will learn to embrace this concept. After all, their success becomes our success.

> "Don't be afraid to give up the good to go for the great."
>
> ~John D. Rockefeller - Oil industry magnate and philanthropist - The wealthiest American of all time

NEVER ask your volunteers to do anything you either have not already done yourself, or that you would not be willing to do yourself. It is way too easy to rely on them to do the 'dirty work' and allow yourself to do the public stuff that brings praise. If you are not working behind the scenes to make sure everything is successful, should you really be the one on the stage with the microphone?

Be willing to put in as much time and effort as they do. Be prepared to sweep the floor when it is dirty. Be available to help them with the paperwork when you can see they are tired or struggling. If there is an event that goes all weekend, don't ask them to work the event while you stay home watching TV and check in with them occasionally. Again, you will only get away with that once.

> "A leader is not an administrator who loves to run others, but someone who carries water for his people so they can get on with their jobs."
>
> ~Robert Townsend - Author and CEO of Avis Rental Cars

ALWAYS, as much as is feasible, include your volunteers in your life. I understand this is not always possible, but when you can, the rewards will be great! Take one of them out to coffee and don't discuss 'work' with them. Go hang out and watch one of their kids or grandkids play soccer. Pick up one of the younger ones (with parental permission, of course) and take him or her fishing.

Let them see you as a 'normal' person. Encourage them to feel connected to you. Allow them to build a friendship with you. Never forget that they work hard because they like you, not just only because they like the cause. Their commitment to your organization will not matter if they do not connect with you, personally. They will get frustrated or dejected and stop showing up.

Any above and beyond activity on their part is a reflection of good leadership on your part.

---

"To handle yourself, use your head; to handle others use your heart."

~Eleanor Roosevelt - First Lady of the United States

---

This is one of the areas that I failed at when I had 450 volunteers across the state. I was a single homeschool mom with two teenage boys, working *at least* 70 hours per week. I had no room to include even my favorite volunteers into my personal life. Looking back, I think that is possibly my biggest regret with that particular job. I had the opportunity to make so many great friends from one corner of Colorado to the other, outside of my work hours, but was not in a position to do so. I knew my boys would only be young for a short season, and that time with them was precious.

Including your volunteers into your life, as much as you can, is possibly the best team-building and fulfilling activity you can do. However, boundaries are VITAL to your own mental health. You must set very clear and well-defined boundaries for your volunteers or they will consume you. They will devour your time, your energy, your joy, and your family life.

If you don't set hours that they can or cannot contact you, true emergencies excepted, they will call you from 6am to 11pm with questions. They will assume that because they are up and working for the cause, you should be, too. You may not mind that from time to time, but boundaries are healthy - on both sides. Your teammates need to respect your time, just like you need to respect theirs.

---

## "There are no office hours for leaders."

~James Gibbons - Cardinal and Archbishop of Baltimore

---

ALWAYS let them 'have a life' outside of your organization. Don't hold <u>meetings</u> on holiday weekends. (Activities that are completely voluntary are great, but not informational or planning meetings.) Don't 'require' them to be at unnecessary meetings every single week. Don't give them grief when they have to bow out of a meeting or activity. Allow them to put their family first. They will work harder for you the rest of the time.

If you know their son is having a band concert, tell them to skip the meeting. Don't just give them permission, actually tell them to do it. They will be grateful because then the decision is no longer in their hands and their colleagues cannot hold it against them.

Far too often, a volunteer-driven organization will require too much time and effort from its people, rather than not providing enough opportunities for them to serve.

We all have busy lives. Your volunteer teammates are there because they *want* to serve. They *want* to help. They *want* to be part of something larger than themselves. Provide many opportunities for them to fulfill those longings, but don't overwhelm them with time commitments.

If we don't allow them guilt-free time with their families, their commitment to us, as well as to our organization, will dissipate quickly. They will be more committed and involved in the times when they can participate if we don't push them to do things when they cannot.

They are adults. They know their own time schedules. They know how much time they can volunteer. Don't make the mistake of acting like you know their schedule and commitments better than they do. Don't make the error of requiring more time than they are willing to give - voluntarily. It can backfire and you might lose them completely.

If they are forced to choose between family and their volunteer project, to avoid resentment and tension in their home, they will (and should) end up choosing their family. If their volunteer time with your organization causes a problem at home, most will decide it isn't worth it. If family doesn't win, nobody wins, and that reflects poorly on your organization.

---

"Do you wish to rise? Begin by descending. You plan a tower that will pierce the clouds? Lay first the foundation of humility."

~St. Augustine

---

ALWAYS practice what you preach. Always.

Integrity is the most important quality that ANY leader in ANY capacity can have. Do what is right, even when nobody is watching. You must hold yourself to high standards. Have the integrity to do the same thing in private as you do in front of them. You must take responsibility for your own life.

The most important person to be honest with is yourself. When YOU know that you tell little white lies, or even big whopper lies, you will not respect yourself. How can you expect others to hold you in high esteem when you know somewhere deep down inside that you are lacking in integrity?

Your teammates will only see the by-product of your personal principles. They may not know that you don't hold yourself to the same bar that you hold them, at least not for a while. However, there is no such thing as a secret. You will be found out.

If we do the right thing just because we are afraid of being caught, or fearful of the results, we are not walking in integrity. We should ALWAYS do the right thing because it is ALWAYS the right thing to do!

---

"Do right and risk the consequences."

~Bob Enyart - Pastor and radio talk show host

---

Yes, there may be consequences when we do the right thing: if we tell the difficult truth, if we return the money, if we honor our word ... But, the ramifications from doing the right thing are usually less painful in the end, and generally result in greater respect from our peers. They are totally worth the initial discomfort.

We have all had leaders who were inconsistent, which is a by-product of a lack of integrity. When you say you will do something, regardless of how difficult it is to keep your word, you absolutely MUST do it. If you say you will be there, then be there. If you say you will provide something, then provide it. It doesn't take much consistency before your people figure out that you have what it takes to lead them to success. You have integrity.

---

"The supreme quality of leadership is integrity."

~President Dwight D. Eisenhower

---

Our integrity provides them with a sense of safety. A sense of consistency. A sense of ability – the sky is the limit. They know somewhere deep inside that we will be there for them if they fail or fall. When they know that we have their back, because we said we will support them - and we always say what we mean and mean what we say - it opens up worlds of possibility within our teams.

Your personal integrity may be the reason why a whole organization succeeds or fails. Keep that monumental thought at the front of your mind next time you are tempted to fib or not report numbers correctly. Again, there is no such thing as a secret.

"You may be certain that your sin WILL find you out." ~Numbers 32:23

We must employ a high standard of ethics in our personal as well as professional lives. Our honesty and self-respect will bring out good things in our team.

---

"Winning is not a sometime thing, it is an all the time thing. You don't do things right once in a while - you do them right all the time!"

~Vince Lombardi - Legendary football player and coach

---

ALWAYS follow your own advice.

As a leader, one of the most difficult challenges we face is that of practicing what we preach. Oftentimes we send the message that it's okay for US to do something, but not okay for our teammates to do it.

Examples:

Standing at the back of the room talking while someone is speaking

Texting in a meeting or conference.

No drinks in the room … except YOUR Starbucks?

Posting on social media during a seminar, meeting, or event.

Showing up late. Ever.

Unprofessional or inappropriate clothing.

If it is okay for you to do it, they will assume that you do not say what you mean and it is therefore okay for them to do it as well. If you say _____ is not allowed, then that means YOU, too.

When we say one thing but do another, we are telling our volunteers that we are superior to them, and that whatever we have to say or do is more important than what they need to say or do. That is a recipe for disrespect and turnover. It is counterproductive, and openly shows a lack of integrity.

**Our teammates will do 50% of what we do right, and 200% of what we do wrong.**

"Nothing so conclusively proves a man's ability to lead others as what he does from day to day to lead himself."

~Thomas J. Watson - CEO of IBM

ALWAYS give others credit. If someone else came up with a great idea that you implemented, be certain to give them credit. Make sure it is very publicly stated. We have all had someone else claim responsibility for something we came up with. It is no fun. Don't do it to your teammates. Even if they were just part of the idea, give them credit.

Have you ever been in an awards ceremony and thought poorly of the emcee because he was getting everyone to clap for others and not for himself? Of course not. That's ludicrous. Nobody will think less of you when you deflect praise to your volunteers. In fact, they will think higher of you and the whole program!

While Brad Kruger was the NRA Alaska Field Rep, he came up with an outstanding idea. When one of his volunteers proposed a fresh concept, game, or plan that was implemented, he would present that volunteer with a 'Super Genius Award'. It was a block of wood with a lightbulb glued into it and the words 'Super Genius' written on the front with a Sharpie marker. Cheap, easy, and rough, but that wasn't the significant part. It was the whole concept of it that meant something. He would present the award at their year-end banquet, in front of all the volunteers in the state, with much fanfare. Many of them proudly displayed it on their desks at work because they were so pleased with their award.

Be creative. It does not need to be expensive. It's the thought that counts. They will love the recognition!

---

## "I not only use all the brains I have, but all I can borrow."

~President Woodrow Wilson

---

Maybe, in reality, you did the lion's share of the work, but your volunteers certainly won't think so, and they will be frustrated and hurt if you take the lion's share of the credit. It will not harm you to allow them to have the limelight and get praised for the success of the program.

On the flip side, it will fuel them to continue to come up with great ideas, share those gems, and implement them for future praise and recognition. It is well worth our effort to publicly give away as much credit as we possibly can.

We should step into the shadows and give our teammates the spotlight. As often as possible. Many volunteers will quietly slip away when they don't feel adequately recognized for their efforts.

My sister used to volunteer to make bibs for baby baskets at a nearby military base. At her local quilt guild, only the volunteer leader was recognized, and she shared none of the praise with her team. Although my sister's objective wasn't for accolades, it bothered her that not only did she get no recognition for the hours she spent, but the leader happily absorbed it all. Eventually, my sister quit volunteering with that particular charity and found a different way to donate her sewing talents where she felt needed, appreciated, and recognized. That leader probably never knew why her volunteers were leaving after such a short time.

Humility comes from acknowledging that your own achievement is the result of the investment of others in your life.

---

"The best way to have a good idea is to have lots of ideas!"

~Linus Pauling - Nobel Scientist

---

ALWAYS brag about your volunteers, but do so behind their back as well as in front of them. The feeling you get when you find out that your leader was edifying you to someone else is downright amazing. It is empowering. It is perceived as so much more genuine than a compliment someone says to your face.

You know how long, or rather how short, it takes for gossip to get around? The same goes for positive things that are said about someone when they are not present. Their friends will make sure they hear about it, and it will do nothing but strengthen your relationship. Don't forget to celebrate small victories with them, and praise them publicly, too.

However, if the only time we compliment them is behind their back, it will destroy the effect and cause them to lose their self-confidence around us. Praise, public as well as private, is always a good habit to be in.

It also needs to be noted that insincere, constant, repetitive, or overdone praise will have the opposite effect. If your teammates can tell that you say the same things about everyone, that you don't really mean what you say, or that it is just something you've been told that you need to do, they will recognize quickly that your praise is mostly meaningless. It will actually become worthless drivel and then any real and true compliments will be missed, overlooked, or dismissed.

Recognizing our teammates shows greatness of mind. We must not ever forget how many people it takes to make things happen, nor all of the help we had to get to where we are now. No man is an island, and there is no 'I' in teamwork.

**Teamwork makes the dream work.**

---

"Outstanding leaders go out of the way to boost the self-esteem of their personnel. If people believe in themselves, it is amazing what they can accomplish!"

~Sam Walton - Founder of Walmart

---

Make use of social media. I know ... please hear me out, though, even if you have to come along kicking and screaming. Like it or not, social media is here to stay. It is the preferred method of communication for the vast majority of people, regardless of age. It is generally FREE and you can reach a far more targeted audience on social media than anywhere else available.

Facebook is where people hang out. You *need* to be there, too. Instagram is how people share snapshots of what they care about. You *need* to be part of it.

Question: How often do people think about your organization?

Answer: As often as you make them think about it.

That one thought should be enough to radically change how we approach things. If we don't MAKE them remember us, they probably won't. People lead very busy and full lives. Out of sight is out of mind.

Every contact you can initiate with them brings your NM business or charity back into their sight and mind. They will only donate or volunteer if they actually remember your organization. They will only show up at your church if they know you are there. They will only attend meetings if they are informed about when the events will be held.

Make them think about your cause as often as is possible! Social media is an amazing and free tool to make that happen.

Let's just examine FaceBook for a moment. You can advertise for more volunteers, announce a fund-raiser, promote an auction or raffle, post service times, invite to a specific prayer meeting, or provide information about your movement, a product you are selling, or pretty much whatever you'd like – FOR FREE!

You can also purchase paid advertising and target those ads to a highly specific audience - such as your town or area, only moms with small children, only men between 50 and 65 years old, only people who have liked specific pages of interest, etc. AND you can advertise for as little as $5. You choose your budget.

You are charged a small amount per person who clicks on your ad. When it has reached $20 worth of people clicking (or whatever your budget was), Facebook turns off the advertisement. They are a fantastic alternative to traditional paid venues for promotion and publicity.

---

## "Don't follow the crowd - let the crowd follow you."

~Margaret Thatcher - British Prime Minister

---

I produce and sell Quilt Fabric Organizers. I target my Facebook advertising to women between 18 and 65 years old who have liked other pages about fabric, sewing, quilting, crafting, etc. It is a very specific audience so my advertising dollars are not wasted on teenage athletes, men who like to hunt, or other demographics who would most likely not be interested in storing their quilt fabric in a beautiful and useful manner. It saves me a lot of money to target it that way.

In addition to advertising, we can communicate with our volunteers in a group forum where everyone can follow the interactions. Posts can be about meetings or sign-up lists. They can be about issues or ideas. They can be another venue to share plans. Your Facebook group can be private so nobody outside of those invited will even know it exists.

You can easily make 'events' and invite people to them with free online invitations. 'Events' can be meetings, fund-raisers, potlucks, banquets, online training opportunities, conference calls, and the list goes on. The sky is the limit. There are a plethora of tutorials online to explain how to make the most of your social media advertising. Did I mention it is FREE?

---

"The task of the leader is to get their people from where they are to where they have not been."

~Henry Kissinger - US Secretary of State

---

ALWAYS welcome, invite, and encourage constructive criticism. Be very open to it. It may be painful, but if your volunteers can air their complaints about you, they will be more likely to stick with the program, and less likely to create dissention behind your back. Most of the time, they cannot go to your 'boss' with their problems, so you have to give them another constructive avenue to vent.

If we don't provide a way for them to gripe, they will grumble to each other. Suddenly everyone will be disgruntled with us and we may lose an entire group of volunteers rather than just one. That can devastate a whole program. Murmuring multiplies misery.

Garnering honest feedback from our team is important, and one way is to offer anonymous evaluation forms to them once per quarter or so. Ask them to candidly assess how YOU are doing as their leader, and provide a way for them to return the forms in a truly anonymous fashion.

You'll need to get alone to read them because sometimes they will be brutal about your faults. But, if you cannot take correction, that means you probably have an un-teachable or un-coachable spirit and you will most likely fail. Not only as a volunteer leader, but also in every other venture in which you try to lead.

---

"Nearly all men can stand adversity, but if you want to test a man's character, give him power."

~President Abraham Lincoln

---

Thankfully, we can all learn. We can purpose in our hearts to become more coachable. We can reflect on our own faults. We can grow and become better. We can force ourselves to become teachable. We can study and learn so that we are more effective leaders. There is always someone out there who is 'better' at whatever we do than we are. We must find that person and make it our ambition to learn all we can from them. The distinction lies in whether or not we *want* to. A sincere desire to learn and grow is imperative.

Always invite constructive criticism and take it to heart. That is a huge step toward becoming the leader we truly want to be.

---

"A life spent making mistakes is not only more honorable, but more useful than a life spent doing nothing."

~George Bernard Shaw - Irish playwright

---

NEVER allow your deficiency to define you.

Do you have poor communication skills? Is time management beyond your grasp? Is follow through difficult for you? GOOD! You can fix each of those issues and be *much* stronger than the person who does not struggle with such shortcomings.

Communication is a learned skill. It is not something that comes natural to humans. Some of us master it earlier than others, but it is still a learned skill. Those of us who picked it up when we were kids did so through trial and error.

You, as an intelligent adult, can read books written by experts and skip all of the 'experimentation' that can be so painful. You can listen to audio books. You can attend seminars. You can watch YouTube videos that will teach you how to do better. Most of these options are free if you go to the library. You can become a far more effective communicator than those who quit learning, growing, and changing when they were teenagers.

We can either allow our deficiencies to define us, or we can tackle them, overcome them, and become far more accomplished than those who don't suffer from them. Our teammates will be grateful to see us improving ourselves in order to make their 'jobs' easier.

Let's look at Oscar Pistorius for a moment. He had both legs amputated below the knee when he was 11 months old. That's a pretty serious deficiency or handicap. However, we all know his name because he worked hard to overcome that and actually ran, at a competitive level, in the 2012 Olympic Games.

Only .000001% of the population of the earth competes in the Olympics. More than 99% of us who have both of our legs won't do what it takes to achieve that level of athleticism. He didn't allow his deficiency to define him, he overcame it!

Sadly, he also committed murder, so I almost didn't include him in this book, but the fact remains that he became much stronger than most of us who don't contend with his physical issues. That is the point.

We ALL struggle with particular areas of our lives where we wish we were more effective, talented, gifted, or efficient. The thing that separates the great from the good is how we deal with those areas. Do we allow them to restrain us, or do we compel them to propel us?

Talent is nothing. Endurance is everything.

Hard work beats talent when talent doesn't work hard.

---

"Before you are a leader, success is all about growing yourself. When you become a leader, success is all about growing others."

~Jack Welch - Author and CEO of GE

---

ALWAYS take much more of the blame than you do of the credit. When things go great, it is to the credit of your volunteers. When things don't go great, it is your fault – whether it is or isn't.

If you haven't checked your ego or swallowed your pride and one thing goes wrong, your volunteers will be forced to take the blame, and many of them will leave. End of story. It's a question of whether you want to take the fall and have runners who will continue to work with you, or if you want to make sure that everyone knows that you did your job but they didn't do theirs. I promise, there is no way you can possibly phrase it where you will come out on top. Fair or not, you must take more of the blame and less of the credit.

---

## "Leaders don't inflict pain - they share pain."

### ~Max Depree - Author of Leadership is an Art

---

NEVER forget to laugh and have fun! People are attracted to laughter and fun!

Laughter is a very real metric to measure the health of your team. Where there is lots of laughter, it shows that people are comfortable, secure, and feel a freedom to fail as well as grow. If the laughter begins to die off, or stops altogether when you walk into the room, there is some serious damage control that needs to take place.

When our teammates don't feel safe, they won't be comfortable enough to laugh. Remember that our job is to take care of our PEOPLE. If they are in fear that we are going to be so concerned with the numbers or the outcome that we forget that they are the important part of the equation, they will drop off like flies.

People work much harder and more efficiently when they are not only allowed to have fun doing it, but even more importantly when they are encouraged to enjoy themselves while working.

---

> "Nothing great was ever created without enthusiasm."
>
> ~Ralph Waldo Emerson - Essayist, lecturer, and poet

---

Look at Google and Apple; two of the largest, most dynamic, effective, and lucrative businesses ever. Their work atmospheres promote fun and creativity. Google's philosophy is to 'create the happiest, most productive workplace in the world.' They have play areas, Broadway-themed conference rooms, chaise lounges on the patios, and conversation areas designed to look like vintage subway cars. The employees design their own desks out of oversized tinker toys. The walls are all made to be written on when inspiration hits. They offer free food and drinks in the kitchen and break rooms. Employees get free massages and art classes. Every single thing about the environment is designed to promote fun and creativity.

Why do we get so hung up on being serious and studious when we are 'working'? Why can't we try to create our own happiest and most productive 'workplaces'? We would get much better results from our teammates if we did. Google is living proof!

It is imperative to have fun in the times surrounding the grind - the times in between the awkwardness of contacting friends and family to sell raffle tickets or ask for donations. Make the celebrations of the small wins enjoyable. That makes the whole project easier to handle and process. It gives us more desire to stick with it. Just a spoon full of sugar helps the medicine go down. (Okay, stop singing and keep reading. ☺ )

---

"If you are not having fun, you aren't doing something right."

~Fran Tarkenton - Quarterback, TV personality, author, and computer software pioneer/executive

---

ALWAYS be developing leaders and training your replacement. You and I both know that you will not be around forever. Your volunteers know that. Your manager/boss knows that. One of the very best things you can do is invest yourself into the next generation of leadership.

If you care about your organization at all, you owe it to everyone involved to be actively grooming someone to eventually take your place. Nobody else needs to know about it, but you should choose someone whom you think embodies the vision of the organization, a reliable runner who is consumed with your WHY, and start surreptitiously training them for future leadership.

---

"The function of leadership is to produce more leaders, not more followers."

~Ralph Nader - Political activist and author

---

Great leadership is about wisdom, not intelligence. You can have a PHD and be as smart as Albert Einstein, but if you don't apply those brains in a wise manner, you may still be a very poor leader.

On the flip side, I've known some fantastic leaders who can barely spell their own name and have never heard of the Pythagorean Theorem, but are loaded down with wisdom and are easy to follow. Don't allow your book smarts to get in the way of your common sense when leading.

After all, knowledge is knowing that a tomato is a fruit. Wisdom is not putting it into a fruit salad.

---

"Real leadership is: leaders recognizing that they serve the people whom they lead."

~Pete Hoekstra - Congressman

---

We cannot fall into the trap of making our teammates think that somehow we have reached some 'higher plane', a better place, a bigger and more advanced level than where they are. We must not make them feel like they need to 'come up' to where we are. Condescension will not motivate your team to excel.

The truth is that many times, all we have done is work longer or harder than they have. We need to always keep that in mind. They can bypass us in a heartbeat, accomplishing far greater things than we have.

We don't call someone a *leader* because they are in charge, we call them a leader because they went first. Generally, they have done things on a greater scale and have more influence. That is nothing to be prideful about. That is the wisdom that experience gives, not book-learned intelligence.

---

"Knowledge comes, but wisdom lingers. It may not be difficult to store up in the mind a vast quantity of facts within a comparatively short time, but the ability to form judgments requires the severe discipline of hard work and the tempering heat of experience and maturity."

~President Calvin Coolidge

---

Delegate, delegate, delegate. If someone else can do a task 80% as well as you could do it, delegate it to them.

You cannot be everywhere at once. You cannot shoulder all of the responsibilities of the whole organization. Part of building a *team* is the idea of delegating responsibilities to others, and then standing back and letting them shine.

This also frees you up for things that truly only you can do. If you are spending your time on tasks that others could accomplish, you don't have time to do the things that you must achieve.

No, they may not do it 100% as well as you could, after all you have more experience than they do. How did you get that experience? Someone else let you do something that they could have done better.

---

## "True leadership must be for the benefit of the followers, not the enrichment of the leaders."

~Robert Townsend - Author and CEO of Avis Rental Cars

---

Imagine you are teaching your daughter how to ride a bicycle. You bring out a bike, climb on it, tell her what you are going to do, ride down the block, and come back. You then ask her if she understands. She indicates that she does, but then YOU ride back and forth, and back and forth, over and over, never giving HER the bike so SHE can learn how to balance and make it work so SHE can ride it. That's ludicrous. However, we do it all the time as leaders.

Our ego gets involved, and we want to show them that WE know how to do it well. We hope that by them hearing it over and over, or by watching us be successful again and again, that they will learn how to do it. It doesn't work that way. Not only will they not be inspired, they will become insecure and leave in worse shape mentally than they came.

Yes, they may fall off and skin their knees. Yes, they might fail several times. That is all part of the process of learning. It is our obligation to make sure they feel safe enough to try, and to try again, and to try again. Our mission is to help them learn from the cuts and bruises so they do better next time. It is not our job to do it for them.

Show them. Tell them how. Let them know that you believe they can do it. Give them the opportunity to learn. Get out of the way. Allow them to shine!

---

"The greatest leader is not necessarily the one who does the greatest things. He is the one who gets the people to do the greatest things."

~President Ronald Reagan

---

ALWAYS praise publicly, but criticize privately. When a teammate makes a mistake, assess the situation, figure out a solution, and don't assign blame. Allow them to learn from the mistake without throwing them under the proverbial bus. Give them the benefit of the doubt.

As an example, last night was a historic football game. The Seattle Seahawks played the Arizona Cardinals, and it made the history books because it went into overtime with the lowest score ever of 6-6. That's not exactly how they hoped to cement their legacies, no doubt.

In OT, both kickers missed field goals that were much shorter than ones they had previously made during the game. In the post-game press conference, both coaches were asked about the kicking failures. How the two of them responded tells MUCH about their leadership mindset.

Bruce Arians, the Cardinals coach: "Make it. This is professional, this ain't high school, baby. You get paid to make it."

The end. Ouch.

Pete Carroll, the Seahawks coach: "He made his kicks to give us a chance and unfortunately didn't make the last one. He's been making kicks for years around here ... but he's gonna hit a lot of winners as we go down the road. I love him and he's our guy."

Wow! What a difference in the off-the-cuff response of those two men. Everyone fails. Everyone. How the leadership responds sets the tone going forward. Who would you rather play for?

---

"Treat people as if they were what they ought to be, and you will help them become what they are capable of being."

~Johann Wolfgang von Goethe - German writer and statesman

---

We must always remember to not get prideful about how far we have come. Pride is a team killer. Jealousy is a team killer. Greed is a team killer.

My Mom went back to college while I was in high school. She is an amazing artist and wanted to finally get her degree. The first day, the professor asked the students to raise their hand if they were the best artist in their family, school, or community. Every person in the room proudly lifted their hand. He had them look around and got them to realize that they were no longer even the best in the room, let alone the whole school or community. It was a sobering thought for them. Each person there had room for growth but not room for pride and jealousy.

There will always be someone who is better at things than we are. Always. As leaders, it is our job to help each person become all they can be, and not allow them to get discouraged when they realize that they are only a little fish in a big pond.

It is also our responsibility to not to get frustrated when they bypass us. If we have effectively communicated the WHY, our runners will be every bit as driven to succeed as we are. If they take off and soar past us, we need to cheer them on! Don't harness their forward motion for your own selfish reasons.

We are not responsible for the outcome, we are responsible for the PEOPLE – we need to always be encouraging the PEOPLE – especially when they take off and run with the vision like an Olympian!

Would you ever look at the coach of a successful athletic team and think badly of him because the people on his team really work hard and do tremendously well? Of course not! Why do we think that in a leadership situation? If they do fantastically well, we look fantastically great. We should never try to contain the serious runners for our own egotistical purposes.

Each of us got to where we are because someone believed in us. Someone encouraged us. Someone went out of their way to help us succeed. For your teammates, you may be that 'someone'. That is the highest praise any leader can receive.

Always remember – pride comes before the fall... ~Proverbs 16:18

---

"As we look to the next century, leaders will be those who empower others."

~Bill Gates - Business magnate and author

---

Just a reminder. As many as 75% of all people who willingly leave their jobs (or volunteer positions) do so because of their BOSSES, not because of the position, the pay, the hours, or even their co-workers. People don't quit jobs. They quit bosses, managers, and supervisors.

##### \*\*\*\*\* LEVELS OF LEADERSHIP \*\*\*\*\*

John Maxwell wrote a book about the five levels of leadership. It is very much worth reading. The first level is where people do what you say because they have to. They follow you because of your title. There is no loyalty at that level. There are only directions and obedience. It can be a miserable place for both the 'boss' and the volunteer. If they stay on for long, it is only because they are on board with the WHY of the organization. It is despite you, rather than because of you.

The second level involves relationship. People follow you because they want to; because they like you; because they trust you. You inspire them. These are the leaders who are concerned with who is on their left and who is on their right. They take on the risks first, and then their teammates willingly sacrifice for them. They admit vulnerability, and that promotes an atmosphere where it is okay to make mistakes and grow forward.

These leaders have the courage to stand up for their people. Only the best leaders have that bravery. Their volunteers know that their back is covered and they have the support they need to take off and really run hard. These are the leaders who actually look you in the eye and care about your answer when they ask how you are doing.

---

## "When people talk, listen completely."

~Ernest Hemmingway - Author and journalist

---

People innately understand that the organization itself does not care for them. That is the job of their leader. When we spend time with them, when we truly connect with them, we will be able to weather the storms together. They will stick with us through the difficult times, and will not be like rats abandoning the ship. We must have the courage to be leaders, not bosses, and they will follow us with gusto.

The other three levels are very much worth studying, I definitely recommend reading that book. (www.JohnMaxwell.com)

Gwen Chermack Hartzler

# Chapter 6 – Lead Like You Mean It

"A jack of all trades and the master of none." How many times have you heard that? Did you know that Benjamin Franklin was misquoted? He actually admonished us to "Be a jack of all trades, but the master of ONE." It is great to learn a little about a lot of things, but it is imperative to learn a lot about one thing.

Mastering the concept of leading other people into success will take you further than just about anything else you could possibly pour your time and effort into.

---

"Become the kind of leader that people would follow voluntarily, even if you had no title or position."

~Brian Tracy - Author and motivational speaker

---

What kind of leader are you? What kind of leader do you want to become? Would you follow you?

Good leaders are always good followers. They have learned how to glean truths from others. They have learned how authority works and have grasped the concept of supporting someone else in their run for success.

> "You cannot be a leader and ask other people
> to follow you unless you know
> how to follow, too."
> ~Sam Rayburn - US Speaker of the House

There are people who are thrust into a leadership role who sadly never learned how to follow someone else. They are the ones who are authoritarian and unbending. They are the ones who struggle with their teammates constantly. Tragically, they just don't understand why people don't want to follow them.

If you don't have willing followers, then you are most likely not really a leader. You are someone out taking a walk alone, but acting like you are directing a marching band that is not actually coming along behind you. Others see it, but frequently, you don't.

People don't want to follow:

- Anger
- Criticism
- Shallowness
- Arrogance
- Tantrums
- Rigidity
- Sarcasm
- Micro-management

Quite honestly, people don't even want to be around anyone with those characteristics. They will avoid people like that, whether they are in leadership positions or not.

---

"It is a terrible thing to look over your shoulder
when you are trying to lead and find
no one there."

~President Franklin D. Roosevelt

---

Here are a few questions to ask yourself:

1) **Do people flock *to* you, or scatter *from* you?**
The answer to this question is paramount. If you are doing things in such a manner that they are moving away in every direction, you need to re-evaluate your leadership style.

---

"One measure of leadership is the caliber of people
who choose to follow you."

~Dennis A. Peer

---

2) **How well do you accept a critique?**
Do you welcome it?
Do you actually take it to heart and allow it to change you?
Do you listen to your teammates when they are unhappy about something, assess the situation, come up with a solution, and make things better? OR, do you sweep it under the rug like it is not a real issue? Or worse yet, blame it on someone else?
    If you are not coachable, even to those who are 'subordinate' to you, you will not make it far. A true leader is not afraid to admit the faults or weaknesses others observe in them. If we are not made aware of

our shortcomings, we cannot overcome them.

"As iron sharpens iron, so a man sharpens the countenance of his friend."    ~Proverbs 27:17

We must be open-minded, as leaders, to let others speak into our lives and the lives of our teammates. Even if they started doing this later than we did, or came out of a different industry than the one we are operating in, that does not mean that they don't have something great to add to the group.    They can certainly teach you about what it is that they know well.

They can contribute something that we could all learn from. As a leader, we have to be coachable and allow others (who are not 'up' to our level) the opportunity to speak into our lives.

The truth of the matter is that often, you have been doing it longer than the others, and that is quite possibly why you were chosen for a position of leadership.    That is no reason to be prideful or superior.

Anyone can speak into your life.    We must always be mindful to not be a 'respecter of persons' and thereby assume that we cannot learn amazing truths from the people around us - who may or may not have anything to do with our cause, passion, or business.

Many of our friends and acquaintances have life experiences that have taught them valuable lessons. They have been open to instruction, and are willing to share their wisdom.    We should always be prepared to learn things when a teachable moment arrives unexpectedly – regardless of who is doing the talking.

"Anyone can hold the helm when the sea is calm."

~Publilius Syrus - Ancient Latin writer

### 3) Are you uncomfortable with those who disagree with you?

No matter how wonderful or gifted you are, no matter how hard you try, regardless of how diplomatic you attempt to be, there will be people who disagree with you. Maybe it is your method, maybe it is your approach, maybe it is your style, maybe it is your ____(fill in the blank)____.

They won't like it and they won't necessarily be nice about it. Do you ignore the issue and become difficult and withdrawn, or do you face it head on so you can explain the rationale for how you would like things done?

Any problem that is ignored is magnified. It is in your best interest to solve it sooner rather than later.

"One of the tests of leadership is the ability to recognize a problem before it becomes an emergency."

~Arnold Glasow - Author and businessman

### 4) Do you *honor* your volunteers?

Honor: (verb) To hold in high respect; revere; to show a courteous regard for.

We certainly expect our teammates to honor us, but do we really show a courteous regard for them? Do we listen to their ideas? Do we allow them the freedom to think outside of the proverbial box? Do we enable them to do more than just show up and do what they are told?

We tend to only listen to the people we respect, revere, or regard. We need to consciously make an effort to be sure we are showing them honor by actually stopping what we are doing, making eye contact with them, and listening to what they have to say. We are communicating how we feel about them and how important they are to us, personally.

## 5) Do you learn from your mistakes?

If you keep making the same 'mistakes' over and over, you are not an effective leader. I've heard it said that things are only a mistake the first time. After that, they are a choice.

---

"Success is not final, failure is not fatal; it is the courage to continue that counts."

~Winston Churchill - Prime Minister of the UK

---

## 6) Are you unstoppable?

Do things get in the way and keep you from forward motion?

If you get hung up examining, pondering, and investigating an obstacle, you won't continue moving forward. Don't let the obstacles derail you. See them, handle or jump over them, and keep on moving. Be innovative in your approach.

---

*"You will never reach your destination if you stop and throw stones at every dog that barks."*

~Winston Churchill - Prime Minister of the UK

---

**7) Are you flexible?**

Are you willing to change direction?

Are you willing to work with others toward a goal that is not your own brain-child?

Blessed are the flexible for they shall not be bent out of shape.

**8) Are you enthusiastic about your cause?**

Your teammates will *always* feed off of your own enthusiasm. If you are 'ho-hum' about what is going on, I promise you they will be ho-hum as well. We may be fortunate enough to have one or two people who will be 'all-in' almost no matter what we do, but they are certainly the exception rather than the rule, and are decidedly not enough to accomplish the goal on their own.

If our intensity has waned, maybe it is time for us to take a good hard look at our WHY with fresh eyes. Sometimes a reminder of what we fell in love with will ignite the flames of excitement again. That passion will re-invigorate our teammates as well. It's trickle-down-energy.

Occasionally, our goals are either too large or too small and that affects enthusiasm. If you accomplished your goal easily, maybe you need to re-adjust your vision and make it larger. If you are having a hard time reaching even your first mile-marker or goal-post in the race, maybe a good hard look needs to be taken in the other direction.

---

"No man can persuade people to do what he wants them to do unless he genuinely likes people, and believes that what he wants them to do is to their own advantage."

~Bruce Barton - Author and politician

---

9) **How much time do you spend in self-reflection?**
The only way to get better at what we do is to be honest with ourselves about where we are at, where the program or group is at, what things could be improved upon, and what things just need to be maintained. A lack of self-reflection quickly becomes fatal. If we don't take a good and candid look at ourselves as leaders, our teammates certainly will. Sadly, most of the time, they choose to do that among themselves and get the group into a spot where people would rather just leave than confront the leader about his faults.

10) **How do you make people feel when they are around you?**
Do they walk away from their contact with you feeling encouraged?
Do they leave with a smile on their face and a spring in their step? Or, do they go away discouraged and down.
Do you leave them with a sense of helplessness? That metric may be the easiest way to measure your own leadership abilities – the attitude of your teammates after spending time in your presence.

> "The first duty of a leader is optimism. How does your subordinate feel after meeting with you? Does he feel uplifted? If not, you are not a leader."
>
> ~Field Marshall Montgomery

**11) Do you allow them to walk in their own giftings?**

Do you squash their creativity?

The fact that our volunteers have been given strengths, drives, talents, and skills which are different from ours should be reason to rejoice. Too many of us in leadership are threatened by that. We feel insecure when someone has an alternate view or approach. We really must get over ourselves and allow others' unique abilities to contribute to the cause and shine!

**12) Do you make them feel like children or indentured servants/slaves?**

Do you allow them to voice their opinions?

Are they scared of you?

Do they trust you?

Children and slaves are often afraid to speak up, they are frightened of those in authority, and frequently have trust issues. Both are told what to do with little or no explanation. Both are made to feel that what they have to say is unimportant.

When our volunteers believe, rightly or wrongly, that they cannot trust us, it is all downhill from there. Everything we have done to build the program; the hours, months, and years of effort are soon to be wasted.

"There is nothing so useless as doing efficiently that which should not be done at all."

~Peter F. Drucker
Author and management consultant

The bottom line is to really pay attention to whether they are smiling, content, and fulfilled when they are around you. If they aren't, no amount of leadership how-to nuggets will help.

**If you don't love your volunteers, someone else will, and you will lose them.**

"The secret of success is enthusiasm."

~Walter Chrysler - Founder of Chrysler Corporation

##### ***** LEAD FROM THE FRONT *****

The character and behavior of your team is a direct reflection of the very best that you have to offer. If their integrity, or the way they conduct themselves, is less than stellar, or even below satisfactory, that provides a view into your own flaws as their leader. If YOU allow corners to be cut or poor habits to go unchecked, you will reap what you have sown.

Again, people do what you do, and not what you say.

Remember, our teammates will do 50% of what we do right, and 200% of what we do wrong.

---

"Pull the string, and it will follow wherever you wish. Push it, and it will go nowhere at all."

~President Dwight D. Eisenhower

---

Leadership is best when it comes from the front; when you are out there doing whatever you are asking your 'followers' to do.

Think of what it would be like to follow someone like Leonidas - as depicted in the movie 300 - into battle. He did not hang toward the back and give orders to the men in front of him. He was the first one out there risking life and limb for what he believed in. He got amazing loyalty and bravery from his men because of it. Be like Leonidas.

---

"Leadership is a matter of having people look at you and gain confidence, seeing how you react. If you are in control, they are in control."

~Tom Landry - Football player and coach

---

There are lots of memes on the internet depicting the difference between a 'boss' and a 'leader'. The boss is always driving the people to excel while he/she is either above them or pushing them from behind. The leader, on the other hand, is down among the people, leading them from the front, encouraging them to do the exact same thing that they themselves are doing.

That shift in attitude moves us out of the boss / manager / supervisor role and into the leader role.

---

"A boss creates fear, a leader confidence. A boss fixes blame, a leader corrects mistakes. A boss knows all, a leader asks questions. A boss makes work drudgery, a leader makes it interesting. A boss is interested in himself, a leader is interested in the group."

~Russell H. Ewing

---

A great leader does not use the word, 'problem'. They do not even think in terms of 'facing problems'. Rather than walking in that mindset, they view them as 'opportunities'. Every time something challenging comes up, we need to adjust our vision to see it as an opportunity to overcome the obstacle. An opportunity to grow. An opportunity for the program to improve. An opportunity for our volunteers to get more involved in the solution. We must erase the word 'problem' from our vocabulary.

---

"Leaders don't force people to follow - they invite them on a journey."

~Charles S. Lauer - Author and public speaker

---

We should also be more concerned with WHAT rather than HOW it gets done. Allow your the freedom to complete tasks in new and

102

different ways. Make use of their creativity. You may be pleasantly surprised at the wealth of good ideas they come up with.

To illustrate my point, let's look at Star Trek, specifically Voyager. In case you don't know the premise, their starship gets transported into an unknown quadrant of the galaxy, and it will take them 70 years to get back to Earth. They are trapped without any support or supplies, unable to even contact Starfleet.

They run into various difficulties and problems in each episode. Captain Janeway always asks for input from those around her rather than just barking out orders. Almost without fail, one of the crew members comes up with some new or different, ingenious, innovative, inventive idea that saves the day.

Even though she has the 'right' as Captain to tell everyone what to do, she values the creativity of her crew. She often tells them, "Do the best you can." It causes them to not only rise to the occasion, but exceed even their own expectations. They obviously feel valued and are fiercely loyal to her. Even though she is fictional, she is an outstanding leader.

---

"Don't tell people how to do things. Tell them what to do and let them surprise you with their results."

~General George S. Patton

---

In order for our volunteers to respect us, we must respect them. For them to feel content and appreciated, we must say thank you – a lot. If we want them to feel fulfilled, we need to give them public praise and encouragement. If we want them to smile, we must always have their back – unless, of course, they are involved in ethics violations or something similar.

Occasionally, we get a 'reader' who decides to cause difficulties. It's rarely a runner who causes division – they are too busy moving forward with the vision. When that happens, it is our responsibility as leader, to deal with them kindly, quickly, and privately. Yes, you can 'fire' a volunteer for the sake of the rest of the group.

My first experience with asking someone to step down from their position was not very successful. It took me three times of telling him that he was causing too much trouble before he finally agreed to remove himself. In the first contact, I explained to him that he had been faithful to the cause for a very long time and that I felt like he needed a break. I told him we were very grateful for all he had done over the years and that we would not be where we were without his contribution, but he appeared to be getting tired and needed some rest. He agreed at the time, but then called me the next day to discuss progress as though we had never spoken about it. I told him again, a bit stronger this time, that he needed to move out of the way to make room for someone else to get involved. He agreed, but then called later and said he had changed his mind. Finally, I told him, as kindly as I could, that he needed to step aside for the health of the whole team. He was very unhappy about it, but did reluctantly give up his position to someone else. The group was invigorated and began to re-grow immediately.

As unpleasant as those repeated encounters were, it was vital for me to step in, as the leader, and protect the team from someone who had become sour and negative. At one time, he had been the backbone of the team, but years of effort with less and less help had burned him out. It was time for him to relinquish the reins.

We need to be able to explain to them that not only will the group benefit from their removal, but they will as well. Some people will not do things for altruistic reasons, but will for self-centered ones. I explained to that gentleman twice that HE would benefit from stepping down, and then, the third time that the group would be better off. Finally, he understood.

When people are negative and difficult, it usually means they are either tired or hurt. Maybe we are putting too much responsibility on them. Perhaps they are having issues at home. Possibly someone in the group has said something mean or hurtful either to or about them.

Many times, it's someone new to the group, who does not yet understand the WHY, who is poisonous. Sometimes it is someone who is there to infiltrate your cause with an end objective of destruction.

Hurting people hurt people. It is sad, but true. When someone is lashing out, we need to figure out why. Finding this out prior to 'firing' them is necessary. There may be a simple (and 'pain-free') solution that will adjust their attitude and keep them moving forward in a positive direction.

Scripture admonishes us to approach them in private first, and I think that is always a good policy. If we call them out and embarrass them in front of their peers, they may very well lash out and cause all sorts of damage to the program. If it is handled with kindness, and always with a reminder that it is not only for the good of the program but for their own personal benefit, most will leave quietly.

Asking someone to step down can create ripples within your whole group, either positive or negative. If your teammates feel that you were justified in your decision, and were making the hard call in order to protect them, they will be invigorated. If there is a sense that you treated the offender in an unfair manner, they will lose confidence in you and your loyalty toward them. Be certain about your decision and the reasoning behind it before you proceed.

If we want our teammates to trust us, we must trust them. Give them guidance and then let them go do their thing. Have faith in them. Allow them to develop a sense of ownership of their piece of the project puzzle.

We have to recognize that they are humans, and not just resources to be used up and replaced.

Realistically, we are in charge of a small family ... or in some cases, a really large family. When we treat our people well, they will walk over hot coals for us.

"A leader is best when people barely know he exists.
When his work is done, his aim fulfilled, they
will say: we did it ourselves."

~Lao Tzu - Ancient Chinese philosopher

When it really comes down to it, some people continue to show up and help because they like the cause and they believe in the WHY; most continue to show up because they like *you* and they believe in *you* as well as the WHY. They like the way *you* make them feel. That is why loyalty is so incredibly important.

Loyalty comes when your people trust you AND when they feel appreciated. If either of those two pieces are missing, loyalty will not be fostered.

The most effective way to motivate our people is by taking action. When we move forward, they will follow.

"Action is the foundational key to success."

~Pablo Picasso - Artist, poet, and playwright

A genuine leader welcomes differing points of view. They are not threatened by others ideas of how to accomplish a task. They do not seek out relationships in which they are easily in control.

We must also remember to push ourselves to avoid procrastination. A leader with great ideas, great talent, a wonderful leadership style, and everything else we would hope for will struggle with every aspect of retaining teammates if they cannot get things done in a timely manner.

We should never put off the hard work. Do the hard things first. The rest is easier.

We should never put off recognition and praising our volunteers. They may no longer be there when we get around to it.

We should never put off confrontation - when it is truly necessary. Just like a wound that is ignored, it will fester and get worse and spread to others. What a sad reason to lose a group, a program, or an entire organization.

In the immortal words of Larry the Cable Guy, 'Git-er-done!'

---

"Hard work is often the easy work you did not do at the proper time."

~Bernard Metzler

---

## ***** WISDOM FROM A CHILD *****

The following is 'leadership' from the perspective of an 11 year old British girl being interviewed by her mother:

**What is leadership?**
Leadership is helping others, particularly through difficult times. They need to show that this is the way you could go for your future.

**What skills do you think a leader needs?**
They need cooperation and they need to make things enjoyable otherwise people won't want to work with them. They need to see people's talents and they need to know what their people have got to do but they've also got to know what they're doing too.

**What do you think a leader shouldn't do?**
Leaders shouldn't get angry when someone gets something wrong on their first attempt. They shouldn't set deadlines then change them to be earlier! Also it's not good setting too many tasks to do in too short a space of time.

**Who are leaders in your daily life?**
You and Daddy, you help me to lead my life, teachers, [long pause] royalty, presidents and prime ministers.

**Can you think of any good leadership examples?**
Mme Axelle at my old school – she was funny. She made learning fun and I would never have gone to art classes if she hadn't suggested it. She sees talent and develops it, and because of that, I discovered a passion.

109

**Can you think of any bad leadership examples?**
My brother's teacher in his old school. She let her
personal feelings get in the way. She made him feel bad
about himself, didn't build up his confidence, and his
learning experience was miserable.

**Do you want to be a leader when you grow up or are
you a leader already?**
I'm a leader now because I encourage people, I help
them in difficult times. I try to be nice even when
people are fighting.

**Do you think anyone can be a leader?**
Yes!

She had some pretty enlightened answers, don't
you think?

***** FULFILLMENT *****

People want to continue to be part of what is
going on if they feel personal or professional fulfillment
from their volunteer or underpaid position.

Did you know that statistics show that more than
90% of people leave work every day feeling un-fulfilled?
That is terrible. We need to make sure that our
organizations provide the opportunity for them to leave
with a great sense of personal fulfillment!

Employees show up to work and often give it
their best effort because they are promised monetary

rewards. Obviously, even that isn't enough to fill the void.

As a volunteer leader, we do not have that carrot to offer them. They must find fulfillment from another source other than a financial one.

- Satisfaction of doing something that they love.
- Using their talents and giftings to benefit someone else.
- A longing to belong. They want to be a part of what is going on.
- A drive to prove someone right, or even to prove someone wrong.
- Competition. Volunteering for a cause is a good outlet to feed that compulsion (fund-raising and such).
- Networking and making business connections with others outside of their own place of employment.

I do believe that at the core, everyone who volunteers just wants to help. That is their main drive. When they are allowed to help, encouraged to participate in the process, given a voice, and emboldened, that brings them great satisfaction and fulfillment.

Let's look at firefighters for a moment. The vast majority of them are not in that field for the money. They have a very well defined WHY. They know that in every situation, their 'destination' is to save people's lives and property.

"We make a living by what we get. We make a life by what we give."

~Winston Churchill - Prime Minister of the UK

Imagine your house was on fire and you knew your kids were inside. Despite the Fire Chief's very well-informed advice to leave it to the professionals, would you just sit on the curb and wait for the firefighters to attempt to go get your children? What if he told you that the building was too far burned - it was too dangerous and he couldn't risk sending his men inside? How many restraints would they have to put on you to keep you from trying to get to your kids?

What if you had just gotten $10,000 cash from the bank and it was inside the house instead of your kids? How different would your drive be? Would they still need restraints? Probably not. Money is replaceable.

What if it was your laptop with a work project on it that you had spent the past two weeks working on? Would you fight them about going into a burning building for it? Most likely not.

If you want to figure out your WHY from a sense of what will bring you the most fulfillment, sit down and make a list of what things in your life would really be worth bucking the Fire Chief and going into the burning house for. Those are the things that actually matter. For most of us, those 'things' will all be living and breathing. The rest of it is just 'stuff' and can be replaced.

In the long run, 'stuff' will not bring us fulfillment. It's not a big enough WHY to knock ourselves out over.

The people who go to work for the sake of completed projects, paperwork, numbers, and money are the ones who go home unfulfilled, regardless of how successful they are.

Firefighters, nurse-midwives, veterinarians, and health care workers are the ones who top the list year after year for being the most meaningful jobs. Why? Because they are all helping people with 'things' that REALLY matter. 'Things' worth running into a burning building for.

It is our job, as leaders, to help our runners see the difference so they can identify how their volunteer position is helping with something that REALLY matters – people.

---

"Our greatest fear should not be of failure, but of succeeding in life at things that don't really matter."

~Francis Chan - Missionary and Pastor

---

Ask your teammates, 'Why are you here?' It will get them thinking about their motivation. Keeping their own WHY at the front of their mind will provide empowerment, control, and freedom.

That question needs to be asked of some people on a regular basis, in one form or another. As soon as they forget their WHY, they will decide it is no longer worth their time and effort. It must always be the screen they look through as they volunteer.

It might be helpful to have people write their WHY down on notecards and display them somewhere as a constant encouragement to stay the course. That becomes their very own personal mission statement, and they can read it while they run!

## ***** INCLUSION *****

Again, as much as is possible, we need to try to include our team members into our own lives. We should try to do non-work things with them. Those are the special times that will bring them fulfillment and build a fierce loyalty within them.

I remember hanging out with the current state rep before I started my volunteer manager job. I was working to replace him so he could move to a different state, but at the same time I almost felt like I was spending time with a celebrity. It's silly, I know. He's just a guy. He's just a leader. It didn't matter. He was someone special.

Your volunteers may have that exact view of you. When you take them out for a cup of coffee, invite them to our house to watch football, or show up at their son's basketball game or choir concert, they feel like they are privileged. You are someone special, and don't forget that.

> "Leadership is not about titles, positions, or flow-charts. It is about one life influencing another."
>
> ~John C. Maxwell
> Best-selling author and gifted speaker

We have a sweet little six year old at our church. His mom contacted me one day and told me that I inspired him to learn the piano because he enjoys the worship service so much. He started taking lessons about six months ago.

I always wave and wink at him, but don't usually get to actually speak with him. We just do a fist bump and keep walking. A couple of weeks ago his dad was talking with someone after the service and I took the opportunity to sit down and chat with him.

I told him that his piano teacher, Miss Diane, who is one of my dearest friends, says that he is learning fast and doing quite well. As we chatted about his favorite song and how many he can play by memory, he barely looked at me straight on. He kinda cocked his head sideways and looked down at the floor. We had a nice talk and I encouraged him to keep on practicing. When I told him I'd love to hear him play sometime, his eyes got huge and he actually looked at me in amazement. We wrapped up the chat, fist bumped, and I headed home.

I spoke with his mom later to tell her what a fun talk we had. She said he was absolutely shocked that I talked with him. He had gone home and told her all about our conversation.

It took me just a minute to remember that he has pretty much only seen me up on the stage at church, playing the piano and talking and singing into the mic. At six years old, I'm sure he felt like he was meeting a superstar! I'm nobody special, but HE doesn't know that, and wouldn't believe me if I told him so.

No, your volunteers aren't star-struck six year olds, but they very well may wish they could spend more time with you because you ARE somebody special and worth their time and effort.

Having said that, we always have to keep in mind that we are not celebrities, we are builders. If we can invest our time and effort effectively into our people, that is what makes us a superstar!

---

"A true leader has the confidence to stand alone, the courage to make tough decisions, and the compassion to listen to the needs of others. He does not set out to be a leader, but becomes one by the quality of his actions and the integrity of his intent."

~General Douglas MacArthur

---

# Chapter 7 – Communication and Appreciation

This is certainly the most important concept to grasp. Good communication is essential to every area of our lives. This is a skill that will take us far in our personal relationships as well as business and civic responsibilities.

Let's imagine for a moment that you are a dogsled driver. You have your whole team of canines hitched to your sled and ready to go, but you don't give a clear command to them. Several of them think it would be best to head to the left. Several others think that the snow off to the right looks easier to traverse. The remaining dogs head straight forward because that is what they have done in the past. How far would you get?

How far would your volunteer organization get under those same circumstances? The lines would get crossed and tangled, arguments would ensue about which way everyone should have gone, feelings would be hurt because the team didn't want to do it 'my way', and you would quickly lose most, if not all of your runners, your best quality people.

Great leaders teach themselves to communicate quickly, effectively, thoroughly, and diplomatically. Those four concepts are essentials. They must be mastered.

> "Keep your fears to yourself, but share your courage with others."
>
> ~Robert Louis Stevenson - Scottish poet and author

If you have read the book, 'The Five Love Languages' by Gary Chapman, you will recognize some of the following. If you haven't read it, it is outstanding and you should buy it. (Seriously. Buy it today! www.5LoveLanguages.com)

I think it is easily adapted to become five languages of appreciation. The leaders who have the most loyal employees/volunteers/followers/teammates have learned these five and mastered a way to recognize them in their people.

It is relatively simple to identify the language by which someone expresses appreciation. Watch them with others, and pay attention to how they treat you.

Let's say for a moment that we are going to put on a fund-raiser. There will be one guy who will show up early and make sure the door is unlocked, the floor is swept, and the coffee pot is perking. He'll be the one who starts setting up tables and chairs without even being asked because he knows it needs to be done.

Someone else will arrive with a big box of donuts and a bowl of fruit for everyone, just in case others didn't have time to eat. They may also bring in a cooler full of sodas for their teammates to enjoy while things get set up. At the end of the evening, they will probably have flowers and a thank you card prepared for whomever was in charge.

The next one will follow you around. They will do whatever you want them to do, but they would prefer that it be something that is in the general vicinity of wherever you will be working. You'll find them sitting near you waiting for further instructions. After the event, they will be the last one to leave because they don't want to miss a word you say.

Another one will be the one who thanks every single person for what they are doing. They will offer words of encouragement and will gush over how great things look and what a fantastic job everyone is doing. They may also be the one who wants the microphone so they can publicly acknowledge everyone who helped in any way with the fund-raiser, and will personally go offer gratitude to each donor from their heart. They will send you a wordy thank you card after the event outlining what an outstanding job you did as the coordinator. Almost everyone loves this person.

And lastly, there will be 'the hugger'. This is the person who always wants a hug rather than a handshake. They are the one who will come up and scratch your back or rub your shoulders while you are stressed out and working on paperwork. They find a way to reach out and touch your arm or put their hand on your shoulder as often as possible. These are non-flirtatious, platonic touches.

I have just described all five languages of appreciation. Nearly every volunteer organization has people who fall into each one of those categories. The key is to not only identify their style, but speak back to them in the same language they are using so they recognize and understand it.

---

"The highest of distinctions is service to others."

~King George VI

---

The first guy I described, the one who is always doing things for the group, is motivated by 'acts of service'. He demonstrates that he likes you and what you are accomplishing by doing things for you.

The second person, who shows up with donuts, sodas, and flowers, is walking in the 'gifts' language. He shows his appreciation by giving things, generally small and inexpensive but well thought out things.

The third person is all about 'time'. He just wants to be near you. He is telling you that he appreciates you by giving you his most valuable asset - his time.

The fourth one, the encourager, is using the language of 'words of affirmation' to express his appreciation. This is usually the easiest one to recognize. He cannot keep his mouth shut. He just has to compliment you and what you are doing.

The last is speaking in the language of 'physical touch'. He wants you to know that he has accepted you into his personal space and lets you know that by touching you as often as he can.

Each person is speaking in a completely different language, and it is very likely that they will NOT understand you, nor feel appreciation coming from you, if you are speaking in a language other than their own native one.

If you present a plaque of appreciation to a 'gifts' person or a 'words of affirmation' person, they are going to be super happy and will feel that you value their contribution. They will proudly display their treasure because it spoke to them. Every time they look at it, they will remember that you spent your time, effort, and money to make the plaque, and that you called them up in front of everyone and said good things about them as you presented them with it.

If you give a plaque to someone who wants your time, or who really needs a hug instead, that plaque will go into a drawer to collect dust. That volunteer will leave the event feeling somewhat unfulfilled. They will know, somewhere in their head, that you appreciated what they did, but they won't feel it in their heart. Chances are good, they won't be able to put their finger on why, either.

On the other hand, if you offer a hug, a sincere handshake, a heartfelt 'thank you' from the microphone, and a round of applause from the audience to the 'physical touch' or 'words of affirmation' person, they will leave the event soaring high and feeling like their work was not in vain. Your 'gifts' people as well as your 'acts of service' folks will both feel un-validated, however.

Inviting everyone back for a wrap-up session (time and acts of service) where you bring cookies that you baked - not store-bought ones, (gifts, time, and acts of service) a hand-written thank you card for each person, (words of affirmation, acts of service, and gifts) and a small gift for a few select people, or better yet for everyone if it's in the budget to do so (gifts) is your best bet. If you can be the one to set everything up (acts of service and time) and make sure there is enough time set aside to get to actually chat with your 'time' people (without letting the others overrun that) and you make sure again that everyone gets *at least* one heartfelt handshake or hug (physical touch), you should have a very happy, very fulfilled, very loyal crew who will return next time you need help.

---

## "Recognition is the greatest motivator."

~Gerard C. Ekedal - Advertising executive at
The Journal of Commerce

---

As a leader, the 'physical touch' people can be the trickiest to deal with. Sometimes others can drastically misinterpret your contact with them, or their contact with you. I would highly recommend that you avoid being alone with ANY volunteer of the opposite sex, but especially one whose primary language is physical touch. If you hug them, make sure it is in a very public place, and that you are hugging lots of people at the same time. There are always those who will be looking for a way to discredit your organization by discrediting you. Don't give them the opportunity over an innocent gesture of appreciation.

Along those same lines, most people function primarily in one language, but nearly everyone can give and receive affection by a secondary language. For the 'time' people and the 'physical touch' people, who are particularly difficult to connect with, it is very helpful if you can observe them and watch for a secondary one to show itself so you can speak to them in that way.

---

"You are not here merely to make a living. You are here in order to enable the world to live more amply, with greater vision, with a finer spirit of hope and achievement. You are here to enrich the world, and you impoverish yourself if you forget the errand."

~President Woodrow Wilson

---

We need to always keep in mind that people join your cause because of the WHY. They leave because of leadership. There are dozens of other charities / churches / civic organizations out there who would love to retain them if you won't.

**If you don't love your people, some other group will.**

Gwen Chermack Hartzler

# Chapter 8 – 101 Leadership Thoughts and Quotes

I have been collecting leadership thoughts for years. When I was doing volunteer training and recognition, I'd print about 100 of them, each on its own sheet of neon colored paper, and then tape them up all over the room. During our lunch break, knowing that my teammates had been sitting there all morning absorbing the content of them as they looked around, I'd tell them they could each take one or two of them off the walls that really struck them. They would then walk around reading each of them with new eyes. At the end of the day, everyone went home with a new thought or two they could share with their team. I got that 'Super Genius' idea from Brad Kruger, the Alaska NRA Field Rep.

I am not sure how to make this chapter more 'readable' other than to just list them. Maybe you can try to 'digest' them in small chunks - perhaps 10 per day until finished; or you can get a journal and choose the three that resonate with you the most; a highlighter is a useful tool; maybe you can just concentrate and read them all as they stand. I don't know. Do whatever works for you, but please figure out a way to actually comprehend each of them.

This chapter contains not only current wisdom, but intense thoughts from many years, generations, and centuries past. The best thing any of us can do is to learn from the experience of others. Here is a perfect opportunity to do so, and I've done all the research for you.

These are not repeated quotes from the rest of the book, and are in no particular order, so the topics jump all over the place. Blessings to you as you glean nuggets of gold from these thoughts and quotes!


\*\*\*\*\*\*\*\*\*\*\*\*\*\*\*\*\*\*\*\*\*\*\*\*\*\*\*\*\*\*\*\*\*\*\*\*\*\*\*\*\*\*\*\*\*\*\*\*\*\*\*\*\*

Work hard in silence. Let success make the noise.

What would you do if you knew you could not fail?

Good enough never is.

People don't buy what you do. They buy WHY you do it.

Great leaders coach others, they do not drive them.

Focusing on your volunteers will ensure a great event, but focusing on the event will not ensure good volunteers.

Great leaders have people who willingly follow them, they do not rely on 'authority' to retain their team.

Great leaders generate enthusiasm, they do not inspire through fear.

Great leaders say 'we', not 'I'. The ONLY time a leader says "I" is when there is blame to be taken.

Great leaders fix whatever is broken or failing, they do not assign blame and pass the buck.

Great leaders show their team how it is done, they do not just tell them that they know everything about it.

Great leaders develop people. They do not use people.

Great people give tons of credit away and keep very little for themselves.

Great people ASK their teammates to do things, they do not TELL them what to do.

Great leaders say 'let's do this', not 'you do it'.

Great leaders take people WITH them. They do not send people.

Great leaders find what people are good at and then put them where those giftings can be used.

Leadership is influence.

Inspired leaders are ALWAYS all about the WHY.

What you do is only proof of what you believe.

Trust and cooperation are feelings – not actions.

Leadership is all about your people, not about your numbers. You take care of your people and the numbers will follow.

Why do followers go out on a limb for a great leader? Because they know that leader would have done it for them.

A great leader takes ownership for helping someone else become successful.

Great leaders are great learners.

A leader influences and inspires the uninspired, he does not threaten or bully them.

Leadership is ultimately about creating a way for people to contribute to something extraordinary.

Accountability is the key. A genuine leader will always allow themselves to be held accountable by their team.

Great leaders don't blame the tools they are given. They work to sharpen them.

Don't confuse bossiness with leadership. There is a huge difference. A bossy person makes everyone around him feel like a child. A leader makes his teammates feel empowered!

"Your attitude is the aroma of your heart. If your attitude stinks, it means your heart is not right." ~Coach Grant Taylor – Facing the Giants (If you haven't watched that movie, you should. It's excellent!)

Leaders grow; they are not made. ~Peter F. Drucker

As you enter a position of trust and power, dream a little before you think. ~Toni Morrison

Doing what is right isn't the problem. It is knowing what is right. ~Lyndon B Johnson

Those who are most slow in making a promise are the most faithful in the performance of it. Jean-Jacques Rousseau

Leaders aren't born, they are made. And they are made just like anything else, through hard work. And that's the price we'll have to pay to achieve that goal, or any goal.
~Vince Lombardi

I am more afraid of an army of 100 sheep led by a lion, than an army of 100 lions led by a sheep. ~Charles Maurice DeTalleyrand

Do what you feel in your heart to be right, for you'll be criticized anyway. ~Eleanor Roosevelt

Always think of what you have to do as easy and it will be. ~Emile Coue

A frightened Captain makes a frightened crew. ~Lister Sinclair

Most of the successful people I've known are the ones who do more listening than talking. ~Bernard Baruch

It is so hard when contemplated in advance, and so easy when you do it. ~Robert Pirsig – Philosopher

I must follow the people. Am I not their leader?
~Benjamin Dirwell

Every time you have to speak, you are auditioning for leadership. ~James Humes

A good leader leads the people from above them. A great leader leads the people from within them. ~M. D. Arnold

Leaders think and talk about the solutions. Followers think and talk about the problems. ~Brian Tracy

I can give you a six-word formula for success: Think things through--then follow through. ~Edward Rickenbacker

I cannot give you the formula for success, but I can give you the formula for failure, which is: Try to please everybody. ~Herbert Swope

Becoming a leader is synonymous with becoming yourself. It is precisely that simple and it is also that difficult. ~Warren Bennis

Wisdom is knowing what to do next, skill is knowing how to do it, and virtue is doing it. ~David Star Jordan

Wise leaders generally have wise counselors because it takes a wise person themselves to distinguish them. ~Diogenes of Sinope

Management is doing things right; leadership is doing the right thing. ~Peter F. Drucker

A good leader takes a little more than his share of the blame, a little less than his share of the credit. ~Arnold Glasow

Effective leadership is putting first things first.
Effective management is discipline, carrying it out.
~Stephen Covey

Leadership is the art of getting someone else to do
something you want done because he wants to do it.
~Dwight D. Eisenhower

The things we fear most in organizations - fluctuations,
disturbances, imbalances - are the primary sources of
creativity.  ~Margaret Wheatley

The art of leadership is saying no, not saying yes. It is
very easy to say yes.  ~Tony Blair

A great person attracts great people and knows how to
hold them together.  ~ Johann Wolfgang Von Goethe

People buy into the leader before they buy into the
vision.  ~John C. Maxwell

No man will make a great leader who wants to do it all
himself, or to get all the credit for doing it.  ~Andrew
Carnegie

Control is not leadership; management is not leadership;
leadership is leadership. If you seek to lead, invest at
least 50 percent of your time in leading yourself--your
own purpose, ethics, principles, motivation, and
conduct. Invest at least 20 percent leading those with
authority over you and 15 percent leading your peers.
~Dee Hock

Great leaders are almost always great simplifiers, who
can cut through argument, debate, and doubt to offer a
solution everybody can understand.  ~Colin Powell

Leadership cannot really be taught. It can only be learned. ~Harold Geneen

Leadership is unlocking people's potential to become better. ~Bill Bradley

The greatest leaders mobilize others by coalescing people around a shared vision. ~Ken Blanchard

Earn your leadership every day. ~Michael Jordan

Great leaders are not defined by the absence of weakness, but rather by the presence of clear strengths. ~John Zenger

Leadership is an action, not a position. ~Donald McGannon

Whatever you are, be a good one. ~Abraham Lincoln

As a man thinks in his heart, so is he. ~Proverbs 23:7

# Chapter 9 – Conclusion

Once again, let me pose the question to you: Would YOU follow YOU?

If, after reading this book, your answer is not a resounding 'YES', be encouraged. You CAN change. You CAN improve. It is not too late to begin doing better. Start today.

There are many tools available to help you improve your leadership skills. Your deficiency does not need to define you. Rather, allow it to drive you toward being the kind of leader that YOU would be happy to follow.

Visit us at: www.WouldYouFollowYouBook.com

Find us on Facebook: Gwen Chermack Hartzler – Author

Gwen Chermack Hartzler

# Also by Gwen Chermack Hartzler

**Restoration: A Tale of Redemption**
Available from Amazon – Kindle and low-priced soft cover.

Restoration tells the story of Liz Durant, homeless and hopeless in a strange city, finds herself face to face with a cop and his friend who want to give her a chance to get on her feet again.

- Can she get beyond her past and allow them to be tools of restoration in her life?
- Can God actually care about her?
- Can He be reaching out to her through these wonderful people?
- Is she really open to His restoration in her life?

Believing that God has forsaken her, Liz runs away from her hurt and ends up living on the streets. In a case of mistaken identity, Liz finds herself being helped by two Christian men. Working her way back into society and finding herself working in the last place she thought - a church - Liz begins to find God's love. This story is a love story - not of just a man and a woman, but of finding oneself in love with the Creator and recognizing His unwavering love.

(Available under author's maiden name of Gwen Chermack)

Gwen Chermack Hartzler

# Also by Gwen Chermack Hartzler

**Jericho: A Historical Novel**
Available from Amazon - Kindle and low-priced soft cover.

Driven by the desire for adventure, best friends Nathan and Simeon unknowingly fulfill God's call on their lives. Thrown into the pagan capital, they confront soldiers, slavery, idolatry, debauchery, and a harlot who is being courted by one of the pagan king's favored soldiers.

Unbeknownst to them, this is only the beginning of their "grand adventure." The lives of these two young Hebrew men are forever changed by the encounter.

Jericho is a biblically accurate, sometimes humorous, and extremely touching narrative that illustrates how God uses seemingly insignificant things to reach each of us.

(Available under author's maiden name of Gwen Chermack)

71926132R00078

Made in the USA
San Bernardino, CA
21 March 2018